BY JAMES KELLER

THREE MINUTES A DAY
YOU CAN CHANGE THE WORLD
THE PRIEST AND A WORLD VISION
MEN OF MARYKNOLL

THREE MINUTES A DAY

Three Minutes a Day

CHRISTOPHER THOUGHTS FOR DAILY LIVING

BY JAMES KELLER, M.M.

DOUBLEDAY & COMPANY, INC., GARDEN CITY, N. Y., 1950

Grateful acknowledgment is made to The Macmillan Company for permission to use the Spencer version of the New Testament in certain places in this book.

NIHIL OBSTAT: JOHN M. A. FEARNS, S.T.D.

                            CENSOR LIBRORUM

IMPRIMATUR: ✠ FRANCIS CARDINAL SPELLMAN

                           ARCHBISHOP OF NEW YORK

PREFACE

Several months ago I was talking to the man who inaugurated and operated the far-flung Armed Forces Radio Services during the recent war. *"Tell me about the first radio station in that global operation,"* I asked him. *"Where and how did you build it?"*

"The initial site was on an isolated island off the coast of Alaska," he answered. *"But we didn't build it. While we were planning the over-all project officially in Washington, the soldiers on that faraway island built it themselves out of old wire, packing cases, and a stray tube or two.*

*"You see, those new civilian-soldiers felt their isolation keenly. The early months of the war, you will remember, were uncertain and bewildering, and they felt a great need to get in touch with the mainland, with their families and their friends. They wanted to know how the war was going and how it was likely to go. They wanted to hear everything they could about it, so they built their own little one-watter while we were planning the big job. Then they asked us to supply them with a steady stream of information and news and with the current **samples** of the kind of radio programs they had become **used** to during peacetime days.*

*"The results were far-reaching—tremendously so. The **men** who built that homemade station hit upon the for-*

mula that we used to create the greatest radio system of information, education, news, and entertainment the world has yet known."

The parallel between that small one-watter and this book is striking. It, too, is simple and elementary. It attempts to help the average person get in more direct and constant communication *with God;* and through God, with the whole world. The parallel supply needed to accomplish this purpose also is by no means dissimilar: a steady stream of divine strength, courage, and inspiration.

For Little People

This book has been prepared—not for those who are advanced in the spiritual life, but rather for lay people who desire to be Christophers—Christ-bearers; to assist them in the daily practice of reflection and prayer. It does not attempt a complete program. We leave that to those more expert.

Much more is required, to be sure, to supply the fulness of Christ's truth which He intended for each and all. This is merely an attempt to meet a *small* part of a *big* need— to echo as best we can the practical adaptability of Saint Paul in his approach to the Corinthians. He yearned to make perfect followers of Christ out of everyone of them as quickly as he could. Yet he realized it was a step-by-step process, as is evident from his kindly, patient, considerate remarks to them: *"And I, brethren, could not speak to you as unto spiritual, but as unto carnal. As unto little ones in Christ. I gave you milk to drink, not meat; for you were not able as yet. But neither are you now able; for you are as yet carnal."* (1 Corinthians 3:1-2)

We have therefore written this book as an ABC for little people who are striving to live above the material and on the spiritual, above the natural and on the super-natural plane of Christ. It is meant for those who are anxious to take even one small step in reaching out with the love of Christ to all men, but who desire at the same time to avoid the danger of becoming so preoccupied with the "good works of God" that they lose sight of the "God of good works."

There is nothing new in this. It is the method of Christ. Repeatedly He used the parables of *visible* things to lead people to a better understanding of the invisible God.

Prayer goes one step further: it is a conscious effort to raise one's mind and heart to God.

No matter how far removed from Christ one may be, he or she is never too far away to *begin to be* a Christ-bearer. By the same token, the more a Christopher brings Christ into his own personal living, the more eager he will be to bring Christ into the lives of others.

The Exterior Depends on the Interior

It cannot be stressed too much that a Christopher's love for his fellow man must stem from his love of God if it is to endure over the years, through good times and bad. And that love, in turn, depends on a Christopher's inner life, nurtured and fostered by reflection and prayer. *"He hath regard to the prayer of the humble and He hath not despised their petition."* (Psalms 101:18)

It is hoped that the simple formula presented here—that of devoting a minimum of three minutes each day to the practice of reflection and prayer—will be at least one step forward in the development of that *interior* life upon which perseverance in *exterior* activity depends.

This "three minutes a day" program is prepared for each of the 365 days of the year. Each daily thought is derived from old and basic truths, often forgotten or taken for granted in the rush of daily life. We hope you will find in these daily considerations something that will help you to pause and reflect. *The rest is up to you*—to use your own individual initiative to pass from reflection to prayer —prayer in your own individual manner.

It's Your Prayer

There are, of course, formal prayers given us by Christ Himself, e.g., the Our Father. But the type of prayer proposed here can be as informal as one cares to make it. Absolute sincerity, naturally, is most important. And as you grow in this exercise of daily reflection and prayer —even though it be for no more than three minutes each day—you will find yourself talking to God with much the same ease as you would converse with a close friend. Use your own words in this simple, intimate chat with Our Lord and they will gradually become your own personal, individual way of prayer.

You will find that the Holy Spirit is enlightening your mind and strengthening your will to do God's will as that will is made known through the proper channels, for the good of your own individual soul and for the good of others.

Regularity and continuity are most important. God's generosity will more than match your faithful effort. If you follow faithfully the practice of devoting at least three minutes a day to reflection and prayer, you will be happily surprised at the progress you will have made in the space of a few short months toward clarity of mind and *peace of soul*. Sinking your roots deep in the spiritual will help you to move from *passive* acceptance of truth to the *active* living of that truth as it bears upon the problems which beset you and the world.

One Helps the Other

Action should spring out of reflection and prayer. The mind *sees*: and with the help that God supplies, the will is moved to *do*. Your every effort at prayer deepens and strengthens your own spiritual power. As your spiritual power is deepened, you will desire more and more to bring something of that power to others. You must strive for self-sanctification. But you will go further than that, in the spirit of "love thy neighbor as thyself." You will want to bring the love of Christ to everyone—into the mainstream of life—*to reach the world with it as far as you can.*

In the Old Testament it is said: *"Remember thy last end and thou shalt never sin."* (Ecclesiasticus 7:40) If someone could follow us always and never let us forget the great fundamentals of life—the value of our individual soul, the deep love of God for each of us, the love we should have for all men as children of a common Father, and above all the eternity of either heaven or hell which will follow the end of our life here on earth—what changed beings we would be. We wouldn't make the mistakes we often make now through our failure to keep our minds fixed on these infallible truths. Instead, the life of each of us would be a living prayer which would affect not only ourselves but the world.

Remember This

Before beginning your "three minutes a day" it would be well to stop and remind yourself that you are in the presence of God; that no matter who you are or what you are, God wants *you*, and is surrounding you now with His love and care. To you He says, as He said to Saint Augustine: *"Thou wouldst not have sought Me, had not I already been seeking thee."*

Such a brief moment of recollection of God's presence will enable your prayer to become the loving expression of loyalty on the part of a child for his father, a child who sees in his father not merely a provider of his needs but the one to whom he owes affection and devotion because from him he has received life.

The Christopher who develops this practice of reflection and prayer, even in the elementary manner proposed here, will experience the growing reassurance that he or she does not work alone; that Christ works with and through each and every one who would be a Christopher. No matter what the difficulties or the degree of one's imperfections and inadequacies, he can help bring Christ into the market place of the world.

In Gratitude

For whatever is good in this book, therefore, we render thanks to God. Thanks, also, to countless persons in all walks of life, of many faiths and of no formal religion at all, from whom have been learned lasting lessons. Grateful appreciation is due, too, to friends, far too numerous to mention, for assistance given in many ways to this book, upon which work has been proceeding off and on since it was first started nine years ago.

Finally—this volume is presented as a Christopher publication, as a companion piece to the Christopher book, *You Can Change the World*. And since the purpose of the Christopher movement itself is so intimately associated with these books, it might be well to summarize briefly our position and our aims.

The Christopher Position

The Christopher movement is under Catholic auspices. By the very fact that it is Catholic, it is deeply concerned for time and for eternity with the welfare of *all* men—of Protestants, Jews, those of no formal religion, and those whose background makes them hostile to religion. In loving solicitude we are bound to include *all* and exclude *none*. Each is a child of God at least through creation. Each, doing even one thing for Him, can start to be a Christopher, a Christ-bearer.

Less than 1 per cent of humanity have caused most of the world's recent major troubles. This handful—no matter what their labels—mutually shares a militant hatred for the basic truth upon which this nation and all Christian civilization is founded (and without which it cannot endure): that each and every human being shares the common Fatherhood of God, deriving his rights from God, not from the State. Driven by such hatred, those few become missioners of evil, striving to reach the *many*, not merely the *few*. They usually get into one of the four spheres that touch the lives of all people the world over: (1) education, (2) government, (3) labor-management, (4) writing (newspapers, magazines, books, radio, motion pictures, television).

The aim of the Christophers is to get another 1 per cent to go as apostolic workers—as Christophers or Christ-bearers—into the same four fields, and strive at least as hard to *restore* the fundamental truth which the other 1 per cent are working furiously to *eliminate*.

It is far more important to get workers of good *in* than

it is to get workers of evil *out*. Positive, constructive action is needed. Little is accomplished by complaining and criticizing: *"It is better to light one candle than to curse the darkness."*

The Christopher movement has *no* chapters, *no* committees, *no* meetings. There are *no* memberships, *no* dues. Rather than have a large number of people "paying dues and doing nothing," we have, from the beginning, set out to encourage tens of thousands to "do something and pay nothing." For the material means to carry on the Christopher program our motto is the simple one inscribed on every American coin: "In God We Trust."

God willing, this tiny spark may one day burst into a flame. Fortunately, we have to manufacture nothing; our product is made in heaven. All we have to do is become *distributors* of a changeless Truth in our changing times, ever conscious that there can be neither peace nor freedom without that Truth which "will make you free."

By your living presence as a Christ-bearer in the mainstream of life, you, too, with God's grace, can help renew the face of the earth!

James Keller

THE CHRISTOPHERS
18 EAST FORTY-EIGHTH STREET, N.Y. 17, N.Y.
FATHER JAMES KELLER, M.M., DIRECTOR

THREE MINUTES A DAY

THROUGH YOU TO THE WORLD

A few days after Christmas a six-year-old boy was trudging down San Francisco's crowded Pine Street, dragging a glistening new wagon with a tiny baby passenger. The passenger was the statue of the Christ Child from the crib of the neighborhood church. Horrified, the boy's mother ran down the street and reprimanded her son sharply.

"*But, Mother,*" the boy protested, wide-eyed, "*I promised the Baby Jesus that if He gave me a wagon for Christmas, He would have the first ride in it.*"

The first day of the New Year is a most appropriate time to express our thanks to God for the blessings He has showered on all of us. Show Him your appreciation in any manner you wish—but *do* show Him. One way would be to reach beyond your own little circle into the big world, doing your part to bring the love of Christ into the market place.

"*By this shall all men know that you are my disciples, if you have love for one another.*" (John 13:35)

⮬ Praying to Christ is one of the easiest ways to become as intimate with Christ as was this six-year-old child.

WHAT WOULD YOU DO?

When the film *Sister Kenny* was being prepared, the famous Australian nurse herself was called in to explain just how she discovered her treatment for polio. Sister Kenny said that she had been summoned to a seven-year-old girl who lived far out in the lonely bush country. The child was in extreme pain, had a high fever, and her leg and foot muscles were contracted.

Sister Kenny had never seen this combination of symptoms before. Hurriedly, she sent a rider to the nearest telegraph station, twenty miles away, with an urgent message to Dr. Eneas MacDonald in Toowamba, requesting advice. Meanwhile, she spent the night comforting the child as best she could. At dawn the long-awaited reply arrived. *"The symptoms you describe indicate infantile paralysis,"* it read. *"There is no known cure. Do the best you can."* Sister Kenny was stunned: the case, then, was virtually hopeless.

At this point Rosalind Russell, who was preparing to portray Sister Kenny on the screen, interrupted: *"What did you do? What was the first thing you thought of? Did you tear up a blanket for the hot packs?"* "No," Sister Kenny quietly replied. *"The first thing I did was kneel down and say a prayer."*

❧ Thy mercy and justice, O Lord, are the cure of all our ills. Grant us to share in them and to share them with others.

NO SHORT CUT

A prominent businessman who was enrolling his son in a well-known university shook his head dubiously when he began to examine the institution's catalogue of studies. *"Does my son have to take all these courses?"* he asked the dean. *"Can't you make it shorter? He wants to get out quickly."*

"Certainly he can take a shorter course," replied the dean. *"But it all depends on what he wants to make of himself. When God wants to make an oak He takes twenty years, but He only takes two months to make a squash."*

Short cuts attract all of us. And of course we are free to take the easy way out. But just as oaks do not grow overnight, neither do the mind and character. We shall have to live for all eternity as we form ourselves here.

"He that is patient, is governed with much wisdom: but he that is impatient, exalteth his folly." (Proverbs 14:29)

Pray for the patience to develop the best God has put in you!

DON'T MISS THE OBVIOUS

There is an ancient tale about a king who wanted to pick the wisest man among his subjects to be his prime minister. When the search finally narrowed down to just three men, he decided to put them to the supreme test.

Accordingly, he placed them together in a room in his palace, and on the room door he had installed a lock which was the last word in mechanical ingenuity. The candidates were informed that whoever was able to open the door first would be appointed to the post of honor.

The three men immediately set themselves to the task. Two of them began at once to work out complicated mathematical formulas to discover the proper lock combination. The third man, however, just sat down in his chair, lost in thought. Finally, without bothering to put pen to paper, he got up, walked to the door, and turned the handle. And the door opened to his touch. *It had been unlocked all the time!*

"Ask, and it shall be given you; seek and you shall find; knock and it shall be opened to you." (Matthew 7:7)

⋴§ Pray that you will use the means that Christ Himself gives you to reach your eternal goal.

A SOFT ANSWER . . .

One day, despite warnings, Donald Carey, a thirteen-year-old boy, climbed over a four-foot fence and ventured too far into an area reserved for two polar bears at the Forest Park Zoo in St. Louis. He narrowly escaped with his life.

The two bears, "Snowball" and "Frisky"—favorites at the Zoo for years—suddenly grabbed Donald by the legs, pulled him into the pit, and began to bite and pummel him. He was rescued only when attendants, attracted by the screams of children outside the fence, rushed to the scene, drove off the bears, and pulled him free. Later, the director of the Zoo said that the only reason the boy escaped with his life, even though he'd been mauled by the huge animals for almost fifteen minutes, was because *"he did not try to fight the bears."*

"Be at agreement with thy adversary betimes, whilst thou art in the way with him: lest perhaps the adversary deliver thee to the judge, and the judge deliver thee to the officer, and thou be cast into prison." (Matthew 5:25)

❧ O God, teach me how to disagree without being disagreeable!

THE THREE WISE MEN

Over the Christian world, today is observed as Little Christmas. The Gospel narrative, the second chapter of St. Matthew, tells in brief but forceful detail how the three Kings, Magi, or Wise Men, as they are called, came from afar to pay tribute to the Infant Saviour.

In their faith, hope, and charity there is an inspirational lesson for all who would be Christ-bearers.

1. *They were honest and straightforward.* Despite the suspicions of Herod, they frankly stated their quest and their allegiance: *"Where is He that is born King of the Jews? For we have seen His star in the East and are come to adore Him."* (Matthew 2:2)

2. *They were confronted with many difficulties.* After a long and dangerous journey, guided only by a lone star, they were met with trickery on the part of Herod, who said to them: *"Go and diligently inquire after the Child; and when you have found Him, bring me word again that I also may come and adore Him."* (Matthew 2:8)

3. *They were happy in their search for Christ.* "And seeing the star, they rejoiced with exceeding great joy." (Matthew 2:9)

4. *Their devotion was wholehearted and complete:* "And entering into the house, they found the Child with Mary His mother, and falling down they adored Him; and opening their treasures, they offered Him gifts: gold, frankincense, and myrrh." (Matthew 2:11)

◄§ Pray for the grace to be a Christ-bearer in all circumstances—no matter what the cost.

IT TAKES COURAGE

A man who took great pride in his lawn found himself with a large crop of dandelions. After trying every method he knew to get rid of them, he wrote the Department of Agriculture. He enumerated all the things he had tried, and closed his letter with the question: *"What shall I do now?"*

In due course came the reply: *"We suggest you learn to love them."*

The Christopher approach always stresses positive action in remedying a seemingly hopeless situation. And if one method fails, try another. Our motto should be something like the slogan which became quite popular among GI's during the last war: *"The difficult we do right away . . . The impossible takes a little longer."*

"Watch ye, stand fast in the faith, do manfully and be strengthened. (1 Corinthians 16:13)

⋙ The prayer of each of us may well be: *"Lord, give me the courage to change what can be changed; the patience to bear what cannot be changed; the wisdom to tell the one from the other."*

FOUR IMPORTANT "ALLS"

"ALL power is given to me in heaven and in earth. Going therefore teach ye ALL nations: baptising them in the name of the Father, and of the Son, and of the Holy Ghost. Teaching them to observe ALL things whatsoever I have commanded you: and behold I am with you ALL days, even to the consummation of the world." (St. Matthew 28: 18–20)

As recorded at the end of the gospel of St. Matthew, these are the very last words uttered by Christ before He ascended into heaven. In the four different senses in which he used the word "all" He was most specific and comprehensive. To disregard or reject even one of these "alls" is to throw Christ's divine plan for the peace of the world out of kilter. That too many people have already done so is plainly evident from the sag in civilization today.

1. *"ALL power is given to me in heaven and in earth . . ."* Anyone making such a sweeping claim would *have* to be God Himself or the greatest charlatan who ever lived. *"ALL power,"* He said. Not 50 per cent or 99 per cent, but *"all"!* . . . Dictators down through the ages, including the present-day versions, time and again have tried to take over all power over the whole earth, but have met with the same result. Their hopes and sinful ambitions have sunk—or will sink—into the dust of history.

(*continued tomorrow*)

❧ Pray for the grace to be an apostle of Christ and reach *"all men"* as far as you can.

FOUR IMPORTANT "ALLS" (*continued*)

2. "*Teach ALL nations.*" Christ didn't want it to be a hit-and-miss proposition. He came down from heaven to bring His gifts to *all* men, not to a particular group or favored few. He meant them for *all*, bad and good, white and black, young and old, poor and rich, and of *all* nations. . . . When you stand before Him, how will you render an account of your part, however small, in carrying out His solemn command to "teach *all* nations?" More than 1900 years have passed and still nearly two thirds of the men of *all* nations have not so much as heard of Him.

3. "*ALL things whatsoever I have commanded you.*" That certainly doesn't mean that one is at liberty to "*pick and choose.*" Christ never even hinted that we have a right to decide to take what we like and leave what we don't like. The hundreds of different interpretations of Christianity can't all be teaching "*all* things whatsoever I have commanded you" or else there would be no differences among them.

4. "*I am with you ALL days.*" You've never heard of a better guarantee than that. And you can't find a single instance in the past twenty centuries where the Master has defaulted. The "going" will be a bit rough at times, as it was for Him. But He is always there, always backing you, strengthening you, consoling you. You are winning while you seem to lose. In fact, you *can't lose* if you stay with Christ.

⋙ Pray that you may always have the courage of your convictions—and that you may never compromise them.

"THE CHIEF THING"

The first president of King's College, now Columbia University, the Reverend Dr. Samuel Johnson, an Episcopalian minister, made every effort to build the institution upon a recognition of that cornerstone without which no solid educational edifice can be erected. In a public notice which he composed and published in 1754, he stated:

"The chief thing that is aimed at in this college is to teach and engage the children to know God and Jesus Christ and to love and serve Him in all Sobriety, Godliness, and Righteousness of Life with a perfect Heart and willing Mind."

What a refreshing change for the better would take place in our educational system if only a few thousand teachers would make every effort to uphold this ideal— at least as a minimum. Each of us can make this possible by encouraging those with sound principles to go into the field of education.

"The Lord hath given me a tongue for my reward: and with it I will praise him." (Ecclesiasticus 51:30)

⋙ Pray that those who believe in God will take up the noble career of teaching in greater numbers than those who deny Him.

FOUR SIGNIFICANT SENTENCES

Basing their authority on God, our Founding Fathers drew up one of the noblest of all documents. In this brief charter they might have referred only *once* to the Creator. But to underline fundamental truths, which they feared others might discard, they wove into the Declaration of Independence four significant sentences, two at the beginning and two at the end. Each specifically affirms the dependence of every human being on God:

1. The first reads: *"When in the course of human events, it becomes necessary for one people . . . to assume . . . the separate and equal station to which the laws of nature and of nature's God entitle them . . ."* Our forefathers emphasized that the natural law itself depends on God.

2. The second is equally positive: *"We hold these truths to be self-evident that all men . . . are endowed by their Creator with certain unalienable rights."*

3. Toward the end of the document the authors appeal *"to the Supreme Judge of the world"* for the rectitude of their intentions.

4. The Declaration closes . . . *"with a firm reliance on the protection of Divine Providence, we mutually pledge to each other our lives, our fortunes, and our sacred honour."*

"God of my fathers, and Lord of mercy, who hast made all things with thy word, and by thy wisdom hast appointed man . . . that he should order the world according to equity and justice." (Wisdom 9: 1–3)

❧ Pray and work that these great truths may be brought more and more to the forefront of American life.

A PRECIOUS HERITAGE

Why did our Founding Fathers emphasize *four times* in the Declaration of Independence that each individual is dependent upon God? Because they wanted to make clear beyond a doubt their belief that no nation could endure long unless it was based upon divine truth.

In the generations ahead they didn't want Americans to forget for one moment that human rights come, *not out of thin air,* but from the Source of all rights. This was no new doctrine for them. They well knew this precious heritage, willed to all men, had come down through the long centuries of Christian civilization.

They were also aware that for thousands of years before—despite persecution, defection, and obstacles of every sort—the Jews had kept alive the sublime concept that man has an eternal destiny, that he derives his rights from his Creator, and that because of this he has solemn obligations to each of his fellows in whom he should see a child of God. The Hebraic view of man's spiritual nature had always been clear cut. The author of Genesis, writing ages before Christ, put it very specifically:

"And God created man to His own image. . . . And the Lord God formed man of the slime of the earth; and breathed into his face the breath of life, and man became a living soul." (Genesis 1:27; 2:7)

⋘ Pray that all Americans may know, respect, and cherish their sacred heritage.

IT BELONGS TO THEM

A wealthy young couple walked into a large orphanage one day to adopt two children. They gladly filled out forms and gave vital statistics, while the officials of the institution did their best to make the visitors comfortable.

Finally, the director, beaming with satisfaction, said: *"Now we'll show you two of the nicest children in the orphanage."*

The wife turned quickly and then remarked kindly but firmly: *"Oh, please, no! We don't want the nicest children; we want two that nobody else would take."*

We naturally choose to associate with people we like, those who are most congenial. But we are missing something important in life if we do not try to go beyond this limited circle. Every follower of Christ is entrusted with a portion of His love that he is expected to share with others, especially with those who have little of it and therefore need it most.

"For if you love them that love you, what reward shall you have? do not even the publicans this?" (Matthew 5:46)

☙ Lord, strengthen me to show particular solicitude for those who are forgotten by others.

REMEMBER THESE THREE

1. Karl Marx, in his *Das Kapital*, expressed himself as follows regarding the nature and rights of man:

"The democratic concept of man is false, because it is Christian. The democratic concept holds that . . . each man is a sovereign being. This is the illusion, dream, and postulate of Christianity." (First ed., ME I, 1. p. 580)

Thus Marx himself testifies that democracy depends on Christianity. To destroy it, therefore, the enemies of Christ realize that they must *first* discredit and eventually exterminate Christianity.

2. Adolf Hitler, who learned much from Karl Marx and the Communists, voiced the same complete disregard for the sacred worth of the individual. In *The Voice of Destruction*, p. 25, Hermann Rauschning quotes Hitler: *"To the Christian doctrine of the infinite significance of the individual human soul . . . I oppose with icy clarity the saving doctrine of the nothingness and insignificance of the human being."* This degrading concept of man, shared by other men besides Hitler, accounts more than anything else for the hatred, destruction, and chaos still stalking the earth.

3. The strength of American life is rooted in Christian truth. As an editorial in *Fortune* magazine recently said:

"The basic teachings of Christianity are in its bloodstream. The central doctrine of its political system—the inviolability of the individual—is a doctrine inherited from nineteen hundred years of Christian insistence upon the immortality of the soul."

≪ Offer a prayer of thanksgiving to God for the great blessings He has showered on America.

NO EASY WAY

A young man, just beginning the study of musical composition, once went to Mozart to ask him the formula for developing the theme of a symphony. Mozart suggested that a symphony was rather an ambitious project for a beginner: perhaps the young man might better try his hand at something simpler first.

"*But you were writing symphonies when you were my age,*" the student protested.

"*Yes,*" the famous composer answered. "*But I didn't have to ask how.*"

The beginner in any field is often impatient, eager for quick results. Yet the time spent in preparing a firm groundwork is not time wasted. Particularly is this true of those who would help others for the love of God. For most of us there is no quick, easy, or lazy way. It is a question of daily plodding, often in the face of discouragement, misunderstanding, and obstacles. Perseverance is the test of our sincerity.

"*And we desire that each of you may show the same earnestness, so as to secure the assured fulfillment of your hope, even to the end; that you may not become sluggish, but imitators of those who through faith and long suffering inherit the promises.*" (Hebrews 6:11, 12)

⟿ Pray for the grace to make haste—slowly.

A STRIKING CONTRAST

Our Lord began His memorable Sermon on the Mount with eight declarations that are a striking contrast to worldly wisdom. Each of these contradicts the advice of those who think in terms of the natural rather than of the supernatural.

1. *Blessed are the poor in spirit: for theirs is the kingdom of heaven.*
2. *Blessed are the meek: for they shall possess the land.*
3. *Blessed are they that mourn: for they shall be comforted.*
4. *Blessed are they that hunger and thirst after justice: for they shall have their fill.*
5. *Blessed are the merciful: for they shall obtain mercy.*
6. *Blessed are the clean of heart: for they shall see God.*
7. *Blessed are the peacemakers: for they shall be called the children of God.*
8. *Blessed are they that suffer persecution for justice' sake: for theirs is the kingdom of heaven.* (Matthew 5: 3–10)

⋖§ Thank God for the comforting wisdom and encouragement He gives each of us in His revealed Word.

MISSING THE BIG WORLD

Some time ago I took a trip on the Hudson and Manhattan Transit System. During the journey, not being familiar with the names of the various stops (there are only a half dozen), I turned to the man next to me and asked: *"Can you tell me the name of this station?"*

"Sorry, I can't," the stranger replied. *"I've been riding this line for fifteen years and I only know two stops: where I get on and where I get off."*

There are many people who limit their horizons as did this traveler. They concern themselves with saving their own souls—which is of first importance—but fail to concern themselves with trying to save the souls of others —which, in God's eyes, they are duty bound to do. They think merely in terms of two "stops": their origin and last destiny. They overlook the "stations" along the way, crowded with human beings who are searching for God.

Being a bearer of Christ not only means knowing where you come from and where you are going. It also means helping others find their way to an eternity of peace with God in Heaven.

". . . and that which you hear in the ear, preach ye upon the housetops." (Matthew 10:27)

❧ Pray that you may extend your vision beyond your own narrow circle.

"NOT IN MY TERRITORY"

A suburban local was stalled by a blizzard one winter's night, and so deep was the snow that its passengers were unable to leave the car. Next morning the hundred and fifty-odd half-frozen commuters were startled to see a signal tower only a few hundred yards away.

The signal-station attendant had seen the stalled train the night before, an investigation revealed. But when asked why he'd done nothing about it, he answered: *"It's not in my territory."*

It's easy to live exclusively for one's self, to be interested only in one's own advantage, to say *"Am I my brother's keeper?"* (Genesis 4:9) But this shortsighted reasoning of so many otherwise good people is the cause of much that is wrong with the world today. You never hear the people who are out to wreck civilization say, about anyone or anything: *"It's not in my territory."*

> *"That sir which serves and seeks for gain,*
> *And follows but for form,*
> *Will pack when it begins to rain,*
> *And leave thee in the storm."*
>
> (Shakespeare, *King Lear*, Act II, Sc. 4)

◆§ Our Father, guide and strengthen me to see in all men my brothers, because they are Thy children.

THE HUNDRED MILLION

Of the 149,000,000 persons in the United States, approximately 70,000,000 belong to no church. Another 30,000,000, "still on the books," have given up the practice of religion. This means a mass of 100,000,000 individuals in our country living off the benefits of Christianity, yet becoming less and less conscious of the great Christian fundamentals which make their present way of life possible.

It is obvious that millions among them are gradually losing sight of the great Christian ideals that have bolstered our civilization for centuries: the concept of a personal God, of Jesus Christ as true God and true man, for example; or the Ten Commandments, the sacredness of the individual, the sanctity of marriage and the home. If this trend goes on long enough, it will inevitably lead to the rise of a new paganism that will eventually remove the United States from the society of Christian nations.

"He that rejecteth wisdom and discipline is unhappy; their hope is vain, their labors without fruit, and their works unprofitable." (Wisdom 3:11)

(continued tomorrow)

O Jesus, enlighten me to do all I can to share with these hundred million Thy divine truth which Thou dost wish to be brought to them.

THE HUNDRED MILLION (*continued*)

The trend toward paganism in our country has not developed to the degree that it is incapable of remedy. The majority of the 100,000,000 Americans now being reached by few, if any, in the name of Christ fortunately are still blessed with an abundance of common sense. Certainly they are neither anti-religious nor atheistic. They are endowed with an unusual sense of fairness and often are generous to a fault. If they are prejudiced at times, that is not usually due to malice: it is because they do not know. They are truly interested in fair play for *all* men of *all* nations.

Likewise they see, as they have never seen before, that the savage forces which have risen up over the world in the last few years to crush and rob them of their liberties have worked even more furiously to stamp out Christianity, because these forces see in it the one great universal cause that champions the dignity of the human being. And they are beginning to realize that the avowed aim of these forces has been to remove the idea of God from the hearts and minds of men, in order that the one and only reason for the sacredness of the individual will be automatically and successfully stifled.

"Observing the crowds he felt compassion for them, because they were harassed and scattered like sheep that have no shepherd." (Matthew 9:36)

✍ Pray to the Father, Son, and Holy Spirit for the grace to play an active part in helping the hundred million to find God.

THE BEST TREATMENT

An eminent baby specialist had a standard treatment for frail newborn infants who failed to gain weight.

When he came to such a baby's chart during his rounds in the hospital, invariably he scrawled the following direction to the nurse in attendance:

"This baby to be loved every three hours."

Not alone do newborn babies need affection. Doctors agree that many of our physical ills result from a feeling of insecurity or loneliness, of not being wanted. True of our bodily sicknesses, how much more true it is of our spiritual difficulties. Love of neighbor remains the best advice—both for our neighbor and for ourselves.

"Let your love be free from hypocrisy. Detest what is evil, adhere to the good. Love one another with brotherly affection, vying with one another in showing mutual regard." (Romans 12:9, 10)

⊷ Jesus, teach me to love even Thy least with the same love with which Thou lovest me.

FIRST THINGS FIRST

It has been the consistent practice of the totalitarians, the atheists, and the materialists to concentrate on undermining, ridiculing, or eliminating the *basic truths of religion* that remind mankind of the necessity of keeping everything God-centered. They know that once these go, all the derivative truths and practices that depend on these primary principles become virtually meaningless. So first, last, and always they center their attack on *Number One Truths*. It seems ordinary common sense, therefore, to take a tip from them and focus particular attention, far and wide, on the following ten great fundamentals which they strive incessantly to destroy:

1. The fact of a personal God, Who has created and spoken to the world;
2. Jesus Christ, true God and true man;
3. The Ten Commandments;
4. The sacred character of the individual;
5. The sanctity of the lifelong marriage bond;
6. The sanctity of the home as the basic unit of the whole human family;
7. The human rights of every person as coming from God, not from the State;
8. The right, based on human nature, to possess private property, with its consequent obligation to society;
9. Due respect for domestic, civil, and religious authority;
10. Judgment after death.

(*continued tomorrow*)

⌇ Lord, teach me not to keep the primary truths to myself; but to do my best to share them with others who know them not.

FIRST THINGS FIRST (*continued*)

The chief objective of anyone who desires to be a Christopher should be to bring the primary truths back into the market place and not keep them to himself. While they are only a portion of *"all things"* that Christ commissioned His Church to teach *"all nations,"* yet they are the cornerstone on which all social life depends.

The hundred million human beings in our own nation (those who belong to no church or who have given up the practice of religion) have scarcely a bowing acquaintance with these truths. Few are bringing them to this vast multitude (and to the billion and a half over the world still in paganism). The totalitarians, the atheists, and the materialists, on the other hand, are swarming in large numbers into education, government, communications, trade unions, social service, library work, and other vital spheres, determined to eliminate every trace of Christ's truth . . .

The solution? Much easier than most think. As soon as there are enough Christophers carrying the truths of Christ into the main stream, there will be a big change for the better. It is that simple. *As soon as there are more people turning on lights than turning them off, then only will the darkness disappear.*

⌁ Pray that you may be an instrument of grace to the hundred million.

WORRY SOLVES LITTLE

It was well past midnight and still the old man could not sleep. *"It's evil, hopelessly evil—this world of ours,"* he thought. *"It's wicked and doomed."*

Then, suddenly, it seemed to him that he heard a voice speaking in the darkness. It was, he felt, the voice of an angel. *"Go to sleep, old man,"* it seemed to say; *"I'll sit up the rest of the night."*

Anxiety never baked a cake, built a bridge, won a battle, or solved a problem. Important as we are, we really render ourselves less useful—and less important—if we let worry stall our action. The best thing we can do is work, with all our strength, on the opportunities God gives us. We can leave the production of the "show" to the Divine Director.

"Why are ye fearful, O ye of little faith?" (Matthew 8:26)

O my God, I love Thee above all things, *"with my whole heart, with my whole soul, with my whole mind, with my whole strength."*

OUR FAULT TOO

A Seattle lawyer once interrupted his lengthy cross-examination of a witness and exclaimed, *"Your Honor, one of the jurors is asleep."*

"You put him to sleep," replied the judge. *"Suppose you wake him up."*

Every single one of us has played some part in the moral bankruptcy of the modern world—most frequently by what we are *not* doing for the common good of all.

Surely if we have contributed to the deterioration which we see on all sides—positively or through our sins of omission—it is only fair that we should now do our level best to reverse this trend.

There is still time. If enough persons with sound values go into the thick of things and strive to restore the peace of Christ and His wisdom to mankind, we may yet rescue our civilization from destruction.

"Awake ye just, and sin not. For some have not the knowledge of God, I speak it to your shame." (I Corinthians 15:34)

Lord, help me to do my share to restore Christ to the market place, and help me to influence others to do the same.

WHAT TO LIVE FOR

In Chicago not long ago a thirty-five-year-old woman committed suicide. To one who didn't know her well, she would have seemed to have everything anyone could want out of life: comfort, social position, and the rest. Yet she often complained of the loneliness that had confronted her in childhood and had followed her all through her life.

Shortly before her death she spoke of the emptiness of her existence and referred to her life as a *"horrible mess."*

Our hearts should go out to people like this. More often than not their whole outlook would have been healthy and normal if someone had showed a bit of interest in them in the name of Christ. But left alone—trained only to concentrate on self—the qualities God put in them never get a chance to develop. With no proper outlet, stagnation and decay set in: pent-up energy often goes haywire and an "explosion" inevitably is the result. Yet many a human tragedy could be averted by a little thoughtful solicitude on the part of some Christopher.

"Why art thou cast down, O my soul? and why dost thou disquiet me? Hope thou in God, for I will still give praise to Him: the salvation of my countenance, and my God." (Psalm 41:42)

◄§ Pray that you may always see this life as a wonderful opportunity to bring the joy of Christ into the lives of those who are frustrated and depressed.

A WORLD TO WIN!

Across the desk of a leading Communist in New York is stretched in large letters this challenging inscription: "A WORLD TO WIN!" It is a constant reminder to him and all who come to see him that there is nothing local or limited about the Communist goal. No matter how insignificantly placed Communists may be, their missionary aim is not for two blocks or their own little environment. *It is for the world!* Every move they make is a move to reach for *all* mankind.

Where did the Communists get this broad-gauged vision? Why is it that they seldom, if ever, take a routine job? Why do they nearly always take a creative post that touches the lives of the *multitude,* not merely the *few?* Why is it that every real Communist displays such driving purpose, enterprise, and direction? Why is he willing to put up with endless delays, hard work, inconvenience, misunderstanding, boredom, setbacks, suffering, and even defeat, in his extraordinary allegiance to his cause?

Why? Because the enemies of Christ have been wise enough to copy Christ's own broad-visioned daring and shrewd enough to adapt to their own evil purposes His command: *"Go ye into the whole world, and preach the gospel to every creature."* (Mark 16:15)

Once the followers of Christ take this important command in the sense in which it was uttered and go "into the whole world" and reach "every creature" with the message of His Love, then—and not till then—will lasting peace be won.

  O Jesus, teach me to think, pray, and work not merely in terms of "two blocks" but of the world itself.

NO BROTHERS WITHOUT A FATHER

One leading magazine editor said that he had been successively an atheist, an agnostic, a free thinker, as well as an indifferentist. He felt that all during this time he had been unconsciously groping for religion, for a real reason for the brotherhood of man. He says he finally had to acknowledge the logic of Christianity once he recognized that it is impossible to have a brotherhood of man without the Fatherhood of God.

1. *"Have we not all one father? hath not one God created us? Why then doth every one of us despise his brother, violating the covenant of our fathers?"* (Malachias 2:10)

2. *"But thou, why judgest thou thy brother? or thou, why dost thou despise thy brother? For we shall all stand before the judgment seat of Christ."* (Romans 14:10)

3. *"For in one Spirit were we all baptized into one body, whether Jews or Gentiles, whether bond or free; and in one Spirit we have all been made to drink."* (I Corinthians 12:13)

❧ O God, inspire me with an ever-increasing love for all men, without exception.

A GREAT TIME TO BE ALIVE

For the next five or ten years, maybe less, this nation probably will be entrusted by God with playing a leading role in world affairs. Which way will it lead? If the Christian principles that have made our country possible are strong and virile among the majority of Americans we may lead the world to Christ.

The answer is in our hands and in the hands of people like us. It is a terrifying challenge. But we must face the facts. There is no other way than the way of Christ. *"I am the way and the truth and the life."* (John 14:6) If we but strike a spark, that spark, in the Providence of God, may burst into a flame. *"I came to cast fire on the earth; and what do I desire but that it were kindled already."* (Luke 12:49)

But there is no time to lose. We must show speed. The efforts of even the least among us can be blessed with results that will exceed the fondest hopes of anyone. God is behind us. He will supply His grace in abundance. It may be that we are being offered the most unusual opportunity in history to bring to mankind that precious gift of peace for which all men long. *Yes, it is a great time to be alive.*

&❧ Pray that you may use the unique opportunity of living in these times to bring to mankind the precious gift of peace.

29

OVERCOME EVIL BY GOOD

The over-all problem facing our country, as well as the world, is materialistic atheism. Communism is but one expression of this godlessness. *Even if Communism disappeared overnight, the problem is still a tremendous one.* An enormous missionary task still remains to be done. The de-spiritualizing process which has taken place during the last seventy-five years is approaching its logical conclusion in our own day and age—world-wide reduction of men to the level of the beast, with resultant misery, hatred, destruction, and wholesale murder.

In every country that the godless have undermined and eventually destroyed, they have swarmed quickly into the main fields of public influence. They have taught millions over the earth to have a false outlook on life, to ignore their eternal destiny. Too many of those who believe in God, instead of getting into the thick of things and overcoming evil with good, have withdrawn into a world apart from the frightening realities around them. For them the words of the apostle Paul should have a particular significance: *"Be not overcome by evil, but overcome evil by good."* (Romans 12:21)

✑§ O Lord, teach me in all things to be a *doer*, not merely a *complainer*.

PERSEVERANCE PAYS OFF

In one of the decisive battles of World War I disastrous reports poured into the headquarters of Marshal Foch, the commander of the Allied forces. The great general, faced with reverses that would have overwhelmed most of us, never lost heart. When things were at their worst, he drafted his famous order which is now in all textbooks of military strategy:

"My center is giving way, my right is pushed back, my left is wavering. The situation is excellent. I shall attack!"

The success that followed the Allied attack broke the spine of the armies of the Central Powers.

There is an old and true saying that the battle is won by the force which stays in the field for the last fifteen minutes. A boxer becomes a champion by staying in the ring and punching right up to the last bell. The surgeon who doesn't lose his nerve, but fights beyond hope, is the one who saves the "hopeless" cases.

"But he that shall persevere to the end, he shall be saved." (Matthew 24:13)

&ξ O Jesus, teach me to persevere for Thy sake, in the face of the most discouraging obstacles.

IT ALWAYS HAS

As William Dean Howells and Mark Twain were coming out of church one morning it commenced to rain heavily.

"Do you think it will ever stop?" asked Howells.

"It always has," answered Twain.

Unpleasant situations have a way of appearing eternal, but we can always bear in mind that nothing in this world is permanent. There is no evil that we cannot attack by faith, by good works, and by our prayers.

In this sense, a "healthy optimism" seems the natural point of view for all true believers in Christ's goodness.

"Rejoice in the Lord, always." (Philippians 4:4)

Pray that you may never be without faith in God's mercy.

SATAN'S MOST VALUABLE TOOL

One day, as fiction has it, the Devil decided to go out of business. His tools, therefore, being for sale, were put on display; and Malice, Jealousy, and Pride were soon recognized by most of his prospective customers. There was one worn, tiny, wedge-shaped tool bearing the highest price, however, which seemed difficult to identify.

"What is that?" someone asked. *"I can't quite place it."*

"Oh that!" Satan answered. *"That is Discouragement. It is my most valuable tool. With it I can open many hearts, since so few people know that it belongs to me."*

One of the most effective protections against discouragement is the comforting conviction that, as a Christopher or Christ-bearer, we do not work alone. Christ is ever with us. We are His instruments, no matter how defective we may be.

"And when it was late, the ship was in the midst of the sea, and himself alone on the land. And seeing them labouring in rowing (for the wind was against them) and about the fourth watch of the night, he cometh to them walking upon the sea, and he would have passed by them.

"But they seeing him walking upon the sea, thought it was an apparition, and they cried out.

"For they all saw him, and were troubled. And immediately he spoke with them, and said to them: Have a good heart, it is I, fear ye not.

"And he went up to them into the ship, and the wind ceased; and they were far more astonished within themselves."

⋙ Pray to the Holy Spirit for that courage which can come only from God.

33

MEANING OF THE WORD

The word Christopher is derived from the Greek *Christophoros,* which means "Christ-bearer." With the aim of restoring to all phases of life, public and private, divine truth and human integrity, the Christopher goes into the market place, into a job of his own choosing, without fanfare or flagwaving. He is not out to do anything sensational. His task is to insist on truth where others are insisting on falsehood. Where there is hate, he brings in love; where there is darkness, he carries light.

The Christopher emphasizes the normal rather than the abnormal. Nothing remarkable may ever be required of him beyond a generous spirit of daring.

He expects to do the usual, not the unusual; the ordinary, not the extraordinary. He knows that while the steady fulfillment of duty often involves monotony and drudgery, yet his continuing sacrifice is ever lightened by a driving purpose. The most trivial and tiresome task achieves significance when done for Christ, Who said, ". . . *My yoke is sweet and My burden light."* (Matthew 11:30)

≈§ Lord, help me to accomplish great things for Thee by doing the little things that lie at hand.

HE DOES NOT FORGET

Over and over again Holy Scripture reminds us of one fact of tremendous import: if we really trust in God, He will never abandon us, no matter what tribulations we endure in our period of trial in this life.

1. *"Cast thy care upon the Lord, and he shall sustain thee: he shall not suffer the just to waver for ever."* (Psalm 54:23)

2. *"The cords of the wicked have encompassed me: but I have not forgotten thy law."* (Psalm 118:61)

3. *"Have mercy on me, O Lord, for I am weak: heal me, O Lord, for my bones are troubled."* (Psalm 6:3)

4. *Into thy hands I commend my spirit: thou hast redeemed me, O Lord, the God of truth."* (Psalm 30:6)

5. *"We are crowded on every side, yet not cramped; perplexed, yet not despairing; persecuted, yet not forsaken; struck down, yet not destroyed . . ."* (II Corinthians 4:8, 9)

&⁊ Pray that suffering and sorrow may serve to purify and strengthen you.

GETTING READY

The life of the soldier attracted Ignatius Loyola when he was quite young. His chief aim was to achieve military glory. But on the twentieth of May 1521 Ignatius was seriously wounded in battle. During his convalescence he resolved to dedicate his life thenceforth to the greater glory of God.

To this end he began a long period of preparation—some eleven years in all. And so earnest was he to fit himself for the task of serving his fellow man for love of God, that he humbled himself to the extent of studying Latin in the company of small boys in order to advance his knowledge.

Even though he was thirty-three years old when he began his training, he did not excuse himself from the effort by saying that he was too old. He knew that nothing could excuse him from doing the work he was called to do. As he himself put it:

"The most precious crown is reserved in heaven for those who do all that they do as zealously as possible: for to do good deeds is not enough by itself: we must do them well."

✍ Lord, grant that I may do something worth-while for Thee, and that I may do it well.

36

RECOGNITION IS NOT EVERYTHING

Paul Cézanne never knew that he was later to be considered "the father of modern painting." Because of his great love for his work, he never thought of recognition. He struggled for thirty-five years, living in oblivion at Aix, giving away masterpieces to indifferent neighbors.

And then one day a discerning Paris dealer happened upon his canvases and, gathering several of them, presented the first Cézanne exhibit. The great of the art world were stunned: here, indeed, was a master!

And Cézanne himself was no less astonished. Arriving at the gallery on the arm of his son, he gazed wonderingly at his paintings, and tears came to his eyes.

"Look," he whispered. *"They've framed them!"*

Had it been Cézanne's chief aim to be hailed as a great artist, he might never have achieved much of anything. But he did achieve *greatness* simply by trying to make use of the artistic talents God had given him, in the very best way he knew how.

". . . Or do I seek to please men? If I yet pleased men, I should not be the servant of Christ." (Galatians 1:10)

❧ Pray that you may seek only to please Him, whether men acclaim or disclaim.

THE FIRST CHRISTOPHERS

About nineteen hundred years ago a small group of men, followers of Christ, were confronted by a great problem. Life was cheap, might was right, vices were glorified, abominable cruelties were visited upon the poor and unfortunate.

The handful of Christians were hunted as criminals or traitors, thrown to the lions, burned, or beheaded. But they were not daunted, for they had determined to change that pagan world by a plan that would do away with violence and bring blessings to everyone, even to their persecutors.

Those early Christians, possessors of the new message of universal love, could easily have succumbed to the temptation to stay hidden in their catacombs, to have their devotions, and let the rest of the world go to the Devil. But they didn't. They took the command to love their neighbor very literally. Fired by the Holy Spirit, they went forth as Christ-bearers, as Christophers. In every human being, no matter how degraded or unfriendly, they saw the image and likeness of God.

". . . *Love your enemies, do good to them that hate you, pray for them that persecute you* . . ." (Matthew 5:44)

(continued tomorrow)

❧ O Spirit of God, fire me with the determination to do my part in restoring peace to the world, according to Thy plan.

THE FIRST CHRISTOPHERS (*continued*)

Constantly aware that their Divine Master had left in their hands the duty of spreading His Word, the early Christians remembered His urging: *"Go into the world . . . to all men!"* When they felt timid they remembered His words, *"Launch out into the deep!"* Over and over again He had exhorted them to *go into the highways and byways.*

No wonder these early Christians left behind them marvelous results, visible today: they replaced brutality with gentleness and love, brought ideals of justice into government and business. Men and women began to recognize the sacred nobility of human life, the sanctity of marriage and the home.

If this handful of early Christians, with every possible obstacle in their path, could eventually remake a civilization even more rotten and brutal than ours, is there any excuse for us today to feel discouraged? If we work half as hard as they did, if we, too, become Christ-bearers, we should be able to restore truth to an unbalanced world.

". . . And the truth shall make you free." (John 8:32)

⊷ Pray that you may make your presence felt among men—for love of God.

WONDERFUL ASSURANCE

We heard only recently the touching story of a young flier who was killed during the war. Before he died, he had time to scrawl only a few words as a brief final message to his parents back home. The note read:

"Dear Mom and Pop: I had time to say my prayers. Jack."

No farewell note could be much shorter, yet few could be more reassuring to truly Christian parents. To them this little message was the news of their son's eternal happiness and the heartening reward of their own teaching, that his last thought should have been to pray.

Some parents think of their responsibilities to their children chiefly in material terms. Of course children must have proper bodily care; but more important still is the care of their souls. Proper care in early life will set them on the true path.

". . . for a man is known by his children." (Ecclesiasticus 11:30)

◦§ Pray that you may always remember to be a good example to the young.

"WANTED: DOERS!"

Over and over again Christ stresses that we must be "doers," not "hearers" only. Vague intentions are not enough. We must use the inspiration of Christ's words as our point of departure. But we must translate them into action, not merely build spiritual castles in the air. Our house will be built upon a rock in proportion as each of us not only *hears* but actually *does* what Christ tells us.

"Everyone therefore that heareth these my words, and doth them, shall be likened to a wise man that built his house upon a rock:

"And the rain fell, and the floods came, and the winds blew, and they beat upon that house, and it fell not, for it was founded on a rock:

"And every one that heareth these my words, and doth them not, shall be like a foolish man that built his house upon the sand:

"And the rain fell, and the floods came, and the winds blew, and they beat upon that house, and it fell, and great was the fall thereof." (Matthew 7:24–27)

≈§ Grant me, O Lord, both to hear and to do Thy Will.

MILLIONS HAVE—SO CAN YOU!

As the harassed driver approaches an extremely narrow pass on a tortuous road in the Rocky Mountains, he is confronted by the following reassuring sign:

"Oh, yes, you can. Millions have."

Sometimes we cannot help but think: *"Nobody has ever been as badly off as I am now."* When we brood over them, our ills enlarge themselves until they obscure our entire horizon. Yet, if we think of some of the things others have had to suffer, and especially if we remember the unfailing grace of God, our troubles become easier to bear. We realize that it is a part of our human situation to undergo pain, and the eternal reward comes more clearly to mind.

"For I will show him how great things he must suffer for my name's sake." (Acts 9:16)

◦§ Lord, help me to bear ills bravely for Thy name's sake.

"MY FINAL ACCOUNT"

The writings of Abraham Lincoln are a rich mine of inspiration. Nearly every speech he made contains evidence of his deep sense of responsibility to God. And it is not hard to see why, since Lincoln himself was constantly seeking higher guidance for his thoughts and actions.

In his famous speech at Baltimore on April 18, 1864, he gave an example of this feeling of dedication when he said: *"I am responsible . . . to the American people, to the Christian world, to history, and on my final account to God."*

An even more famous reference to the Deity occurs in the last sentence of his immortal Gettysburg Address. The initial draft of this speech, however, did not include the words *"under God."* It was only as he was actually delivering his address that he spontaneously put them in. It was as if he suddenly sensed the incompleteness of his remarks and, with that last and most meaningful addition, gave his speech—and our country—its proper direction.

". . . and that this nation, under God, shall have a new birth of freedom—and that government of the people, by the people, for the people, shall not perish from the earth."

"The power of the earth is in the hand of God." (Ecclesiasticus 10:4)

⊷§ Pray that you always recognize that your final responsibility is to God.

LIGHT FOR OUR DARKNESS

Sir William Blackstone, the great English jurist, writing in his *Commentaries on the Laws of England* in 1769, was most explicit in emphasizing the weakness of man's nature. As he observed:

"... *if our reason were always, as in our first ancestor before his transgression, clear and perfect, unruffled by passions, unclouded by prejudice, unimpaired by disease or intemperance, the task would be pleasant and easy; we should need no other guide but this. But every man now finds the contrary in his own experience; that his reason is corrupt, and his understanding full of ignorance and error.*"

At the same time Blackstone points out how God is constantly endeavoring to supply what is lacking in man; for he goes on to say:

"*This has given manifold occasion for the benign interposition of divine Providence, which, in compassion to the frailty, the imperfection, and the blindness of human reason, hath been pleased at sundry times and in divers manners, to discover and enforce its laws by an immediate and direct revelation. The doctrines thus delivered we call the revealed or divine law . . .*"

"*Without Me, you can do nothing.*" (John 15:5)

&5 To my feeble efforts add Thy strength and power, O God.

ON VALENTINE'S DAY

St. Valentine's Day is a good day to reflect on the sacredness of the marriage bond. A portion from the lesson preceding the wedding ceremony, for instance, is worth a bit of prayerful contemplation because in it is a reminder that there is a "give" as well as "take" in every happy marriage.

"And so you begin your married life by the voluntary and complete surrender of your individual lives in the interest of that deeper and wider life which you are to have in common. Henceforth you will belong entirely to each other; you will be one in mind, one in heart, and one in affections. And whatever sacrifices you may hereafter be required to make to preserve this mutual life, always make them generously.

"Sacrifice is usually difficult and irksome. Only love can make it easy; and perfect love can make it a joy. We are willing to give in proportion as we love. And when love is perfect, the sacrifice is complete.

"God so loved the world that He gave His Only begotten Son; and the Son so loved us that He gave Himself for our salvation."

"What therefore God hath joined together, let not man put asunder." (Mark 10:9)

⋙ Always pray for the love that makes sacrifice a joy.

THE GREATEST EMPIRE

Napoleon, in his lonely exile on St. Helena, had much time for thought. And some of his reflections were highly interesting. This one, for instance:

"Alexander, Ceasar, Charlemagne, and I founded great empires. But upon what did the creation of our genius depend? Upon force. Jesus alone founded his empire upon love, and to this very day millions would die for him."

Forcing none, Christ taught in a new way, the only one throughout history whose whole school and whole plan were founded on love. The world had never before heard of this love. And even now, nineteen centuries later, more than half the world is still ignorant of it. Often Jesus seems to lose, but in reality He always wins—and always by love.

"A new commandment I give unto you: that you love one another, as I have loved you . . ." (John 13:34)

⋙O God, I wish to love Thee as Thou wouldst have me love.

THEY DIDN'T FLINCH

The Huron Indians, who occupied part of what is now New York State when it was still a wilderness, gave violent reception to some of the missioners from Europe who came among them. But to two of these missioners, Fathers Brébeuf and Lalemant, both Frenchmen, they paid a strange compliment indeed. After subjecting them to the most horrible tortures, they tore out their hearts, ate them, and drank their warm blood. Why? Because their courage so impressed them that they wished, by drinking their blood, to have instilled in them some of the bravery of the men they put to death.

What first moved the Hurons to treat these two as they did? It wasn't the courage of Brébeuf and Lalemant alone. It was the cumulative effect of the fortitude of those missioners who had gone before them . . . Isaac Jogues, René Goupil, and the rest. Their sufferings were almost unbelievable. They were beaten with knotted sticks, their hair, beards, fingernails were torn out, their fingers chewed off at the ends.

Yet they bore all this for love of God and the Indians, in whom they saw the image and likeness of God. From their sufferings came forth the flowering of faith. In death they were victorious. A powerful example to fortify Christophers when faced with suffering!

"Then shall they deliver you up to be afflicted, and shall put you to death: and you shall be hated by all nations for My sake." (Matthew 24:9)

~§ Pray for the grace to bear all things for the love of Christ.

KNOWING IS NOT ENOUGH

It isn't enough merely to know the truth. We have a personal obligation to spread it. Each of us has a definite role in God's plan to change the world for the better. Each has a mission in life that is more than saving himself alone.

1. "*To him therefore who knoweth to do good, and doth it not, to him it is sin.*" (James 4:17)

2. "*Not every one that saith to me, Lord, Lord, shall enter into the kingdom of heaven, but he that doth the will of my Father who is in heaven, he shall enter into the kingdom of heaven.* (Matthew 8:21)

3. "*I am the true vine; and my Father is the husbandman. Every branch in me, that beareth no fruit, he will take away; and every one that beareth fruit, he will purge it, that it may bring forth more fruit.*" (John 15: 1, 2)

4. "*For now the axe is laid to the root of the trees. Every tree therefore that doth not yield good fruit, shall be cut down, and cast into the fire.*" (Matthew 3: 10)

5. "*Wherefore, brethren, labor the more, that by good works you may make sure your calling and election. For doing these things, you shall not sin at any time. For so an entrance shall be ministered to you abundantly into the everlasting kingdom of our Lord and Saviour Jesus Christ.*" (II Peter 1: 10, 11)

Grant me the will to practice what I know to be the Truth.

A SURE WAY TO FAIL

Newsweek magazine in a brief article under the heading, *"The Hard Road to Ruin,"* recently listed a number of sure-fire ways to ruin a business career and become an outstanding failure. Among these were the following:

"If a subordinate makes a mistake, let him have both barrels, preferably in front of others.

"Never accept responsibility for a decision if you can possibly avoid it.

"Develop your ability to pass the buck—take private lessons at night if need be.

"Be so impatient for advancement that you fail to learn what your present job has to teach."

The same means of achieving failure in a business career can be paralleled in many other walks of life. An unwillingness to accept personal responsibility and to disagree without becoming disagreeable are certain means of antagonizing those whom we, with a Christopher purpose, may wish to guide. Similarly, a reluctance to learn how to handle a given situation invariably does untold damage.

A Christopher will derive a lesson from these faults. He will learn it well, because his sincerity in becoming more Christlike will be the ultimate measure of his eternal success.

↪ O Lord, teach me never to shirk responsibility.

NO SECOND EDITION

In the early nineteenth century the poet John Clare wrote ironically: *"If life had a second edition, how I would correct the proofs!"*

We all of us have but one "turn at bat" here on earth to prepare for eternity. Yet, while on earth we *can learn* from our past mistakes, can avoid making them in the future, and can fill our lives with concern for the spiritual and material welfare of others as well as ourselves.

Those who strive to carry Christ into the dust and heat of the market place will have with them the Light which will illumine the road to eternal salvation. Mistakes they may make, but with Him to guide them, they will never wander very far from His Peace and Truth.

"So also you now indeed have sorrow; but I will see you again, and your heart shall rejoice; and your joy no man shall take from you." (John 16:22)

&S Lord, be my help. Lord, be my strength.

A LITTLE BLACK BOOK

A woman in California was the object of much curiosity in her neighborhood because of a most unusual habit. Every time she went into a store or a shop or a movie theater she would take a little black book out of her purse and write in it. *"Do you keep a record of everything you spend?"* someone finally asked her.

"Oh no," she replied. *"I only keep a list of what I buy in the way of luxuries . . . perfumes, cigarettes, things like that."*

"But what do you use the list for?" came back the query.

"Well, the fact is," this woman answered, *"I feel so selfish enjoying my many comforts when there is so much suffering in the world. So I keep this list, and whenever I spend money for my own comfort, I give a like amount to charity for the homeless or the sick."*

She had found her own way of looking at the world's misery. It is a good way, for the pain of one person is the pain of us all.

". . . all mankind's concern is charity." (Alexander Pope)

⋙ Lord, grant that I may be personally concerned with the miseries of men everywhere.

A NEEDED REMINDER

When conquering proconsuls returned to pagan Rome to celebrate their triumph, custom was to assign each of them a slave whose only function was to remind the conqueror constantly that the greatest human glory passes quickly. This slave would crouch in the victorious warrior's chariot, whispering as the conqueror rode along triumphantly: *"Remember . . . remember thou art mortal."*

Because these proconsuls were never allowed to forget this sobering fact, they saved themselves much of the grief that usually engulfs successful people who lose a sense of perspective. As one historian remarked: *"Thus were swelled heads and rash, prideful deeds averted by an art now all but lost."*

Several centuries before the coming of Christ a divinely inspired writer in Jerusalem gave a far more significant reminder when he warned: *"In all thy works remember thy last end, and thou shalt never sin."* (Ecclesiasticus 7:40) His admonition, which should make anyone pause and think, goes far beyond the natural and temporal into the supernatural and eternal.

◆§ Lord help me to keep in mind the brevity of life and my last end.

ASH WEDNESDAY

At the beginning of the Lenten season it is appropriate to give some thought to the significance of man's origin. We indeed had a humble beginning for, as the Bible states: *"And the Lord God formed man of the slime of the earth."* That is why, on Ash Wednesday, our foreheads are smudged with a bit of ashes to remind us that: *"Dust thou art, and into dust thou shalt return."* (Genesis 3:19)

But more important is the rest of the narrative: *". . . and breathed into his face the breath of life, and man became a living soul."*

Penance, as Lent reminds us, is mortification of our bodies and is an excellent means to emphasize our spiritual nature, our divine origin.

It is a joyous thing to realize that we were shaped by God, filled by Him with *"the breath of life."* The knowledge that we are *"living souls,"* not just *"higher animals,"* should give us the power to develop within ourselves that spirit which dwells there.

"And God created man to his own image: to the image of God he created him." (Genesis 1:27)

⚜ Pray always that you may keep the things of the spirit above those of the body.

SMALL COMPROMISES, TRIVIAL EVASIONS

Recently a large group of "problem" children were given the assignment of writing essays on the difficulties they had with their parents. The papers they turned in were misspelled but lively, listing a number of rather expectable faults—gushing, nagging, refusing affection, and so on. But oddly enough the quality most children felt their parents lacked was *truthfulness*.

None of us, of course, likes to think of himself as a liar. In important things we make it a point to be scrupulously honest. But if we examine our daily lives closely we may find dozens of examples of small compromises, trivial evasions.

These seemingly unimportant deceits should be guarded against, since they can all too easily become a part of the fabric of our existence, influencing our relationships with others. An unflagging desire for truth in every aspect of our behavior does much to provide that sense of security for which all people yearn.

"In nowise speak against the truth, but be ashamed of the lie of thy ignorance." (Ecclesiasticus 4:30)

O God of Truth, grant me that delicate sense of honesty which will help me to avoid all deceit.

"THEY LABOR IN VAIN"

In 1787, when difficulties arose at the Constitutional Convention in Philadelphia, Benjamin Franklin addressed George Washington, the chairman, in these words: *"The small progress we have made . . . is, methinks, a melancholy proof of the imperfection of the human understanding . . . I have lived, Sir, a long time; and the longer I live, the more convincing proofs I see of this truth, that GOD governs in the affairs of men. And if a sparrow cannot fall to the ground without His notice, is it probable that an empire can rise without His aid? We have been assured, Sir, in the Sacred Writings, that 'except the Lord build the House, they labor in vain that built it.' I firmly believe this; and I also believe that, without His concurring aid, we shall succeed in this political building no better than the builders of Babel."*

The sense of dependence on God that motivated the founders of our country should be a characteristic of every true American today—tomorrow—always!

"Unless the Lord build the house, they labour in vain that build it. Unless the Lord keep the city, he watcheth in vain that keepeth it." (Psalm 126:1)

❧ Pray that we may always work to preserve the democracy that God's Providence has given us.

THE LADY WITH THE LAMP

The example of Florence Nightingale is a good one for Christophers. Born to comfort and social position, she gave up everything to serve those who needed her help. The inspiring words of her "Pledge" are worth reflection:

"I solemnly pledge myself before God and in the presence of this assembly:

To pass my life in purity and to practice my profession faithfully.

I will abstain from whatever is deleterious and mischievous, and will not take or knowingly administer any harmful drug.

I will do all in my power to elevate the standard of my profession, and will hold in confidence all personal matters committed to my keeping and all family affairs coming to my knowledge in the practice of my profession.

With loyalty will I endeavor to aid the physician in his work, and devote myself to the welfare of those committed to my care."

"For I was . . . sick, and you visited me . . ." (Matthew 25:3–36)

&⸬ Dear God, give every nurse the appreciation and consolation of her sacred profession.

FOR GOD NOTHING IS IMPOSSIBLE

Christopher Columbus, in a letter addressed to Ferdinand and Isabella, the King and Queen of Spain, revealed the providential guidance which brought about his discovery of America. Columbus wrote:

"... *But these great and marvelous results are not to be attributed to any merit of mine, but to the holy Christian faith, and to the piety and religion of our Sovereigns; for that which the unaided intellect of man could not compass, the spirit of God has granted to human exertions, for God is wont to hear the prayers of His servants who love His precepts even to the performance of apparent impossibilities ..."*

"*Therefore, let the King and Queen, our princes and their most happy kingdoms, and all the other provinces of Christendom, render thanks to our Lord and Saviour Jesus Christ, who has granted us so great a victory ...*"

"*Thanks be to God for his unspeakable gift.*" (II Corinthians 9:15)

⊸§ Pray that you will always render thanks to God for the blessings and favors he has bestowed upon you.

A MATTER OF INTENTION

A sea captain, long noted for his rigid discipline, once came upon his first mate lying drunk. To settle an old score, the captain wrote in the logbook: *"Last night First Mate Johnson intoxicated."*

The entry rankled, and Johnson waited for revenge. Finally the chance came when he was assigned to write several entries in the log. Then, with a bold hand, he wrote: *"Captain Smith not drunk tonight."*

Some of us might have a literal point of view about the truth, and say that, after all, the mate had only written what was true about the captain. But the fact is he told the truth with every intention of deceiving. It takes quite a stretch of imagination, therefore, to believe we can do right *when our intention is to do wrong.*

"They that were of good understanding in words have also done wisely themselves; and have understood truth and justice, and have poured forth proverbs and judgments." (Ecclesiasticus 18:29)

Teach me, O God, never to use the truth to defeat the Truth.

ONE SMALL VOICE

One of the big surprises of the 1946 opening session of the UN General Assembly in New York was a forthright statement by C. Abayomi Cassell, the delegate from Liberia.

"*Every single human creature is the object of God's interest and care,*" he frankly stated, then added that there would be no chance of lasting peace "*so long as one shred of injustice exists on the globe.*"

"*I believe,*" he continued, "*that each time . . . one group of people or one nation takes advantage of the other, retribution follows either from within or from without for that breach of the perfect law of God as well as those of mankind, [which are] products of the Divine within man!*"

True, this was only one small voice; but the courageous frankness of this Liberian delegate brought a sobering reminder into the UN and won from the body of the Assembly one of the most enthusiastic receptions ever accorded any delegate.

"*And all things that are done, God will bring into judgment for every error, whether it be good or evil.*" (Ecclesiastes 12:14)

⋙ Pray that you may have a deepened understanding of His mysterious law which commands love and makes injustice punish itself.

59

GET ON THE JOB!

A friend of ours, whose grandmother was an Iowa pioneer, reports that she was always the energetic type. He remembers that when as a youngster he spent summers on her farm, she would say, *"Here it is Monday morning; tomorrow will be Tuesday, and the next day Wednesday. The whole week's half gone, and nothing done yet! Hurry up and get out in the fields!"*

Those who are blessed with the precious gifts of faith, hope, and charity, and who are determined to share them with others—not keep them for themselves—are usually hard workers. The more they do, the more they seem able to take on.

Isn't it one of the outstanding characteristics of the successful man that he never wastes time? He treats a minute as some treat an hour—sometimes even more respectfully. That is why he gets things accomplished. Success in any aspect of life—material or spiritual—comes to those who are not time-servers, but who make time serve them.

"I must do the works of Him who sent me, while it is day; night is coming when no one can work." (John 9:4)

&ᒥ Pray that you may live as though each moment were your first and your last moment on earth.

NO AUTOMATIC CHAMPION

When Babe Didrickson Zaharias, often called the "athletic phenomenon of all time," won the British woman's golf championship, people said of her what they had said many times before: *"Oh, she's an automatic champion, a natural athlete."* But the facts tell a different story.

"When Babe started golfing in earnest thirteen years ago," a recent article stated, *"she hit as many as 1,000 balls in one afternoon, playing until her hands were so sore they had to be taped."*

Work—hard work—is the lot that God intended for all of us in this life. It is only through unremitting effort and sacrifice that most people achieve success in this life or the next. In a particular way, one who works for the common good of all must, as a great poet said, *"scorn delights, and live laborious days."* Yet, paradoxically enough, one who does that experiences the *real* joy of living.

". . . the kingdom of heaven suffereth violence, and the violent bear it away." (Matthew 11:12)

⋖§ Almighty God, grant that as Thy Son gave an example of diligence in His work as a Carpenter of Nazareth, so might we follow His example in working for the good of all.

GOOD IN EVERYONE

"There is no surprise more magical than the surprise of being loved," Charles Morgan once said. *"It is the finger of God on a man's shoulder."*

There's a bit of nobility in the worst of human beings because all are made in God's image and that image can never be completely effaced or lost. Even the man who has decided to have nothing whatsoever to do with God isn't frozen in that state of mind. Deep in the roots of his being—just because he is created in the Divine image— there is an ever-present tug toward his Maker.

It is the privilege of Christophers to help him become aware of this tremendous attraction. They can honestly say to anyone, with little danger of hurting his feelings: *"There's a lot of good in you!"* With a kind word or a friendly glance they can do much to inspire confidence. They never write anybody off!

No matter how desperate the case, no matter how ignoble the character, theirs is the unshakable conviction that there is always hope!

"By this shall all men know that you are my disciples, if you have love one for another." (John 13:35)

O Lord, help us to see Thy image in each human being and to love him because he was made by Thee and for Thee.

A HEARTENING SIGN

When three-year-old Kathy Fiscus stumbled into an abandoned well while playing in a vacant lot in San Marino, California, the entire nation suddenly became concerned about her fate. As one paper, the Cincinnati Post, editorialized: *"Parents who never heard of San Marino sat with Kathy's mother and father . . . and helped them to pray."* And, at the scene of the tragedy, men who were total strangers to the Fiscus family risked their lives and worked around the clock in a desperate effort to save her life. Meanwhile, some 15,000 people kept constant vigil at the well, praying for the life of the child.

What an eloquent tribute it is to the Christian background of our civilization that people are still so concerned with the sacred worth of each human being, no matter how insignificant. It is indeed a heartening sign; yet knowledge of it should not lull us into a false sense of complacency. Much still remains to be done to restore and deepen the spiritual foundations upon which this nation and the rest of the civilized world rest, and which the godless are intent on destroying.

"Amen, I say to you, as long as you did it to one of these my least brethren, you did it to me." (Matthew 25:40)

&ipp; O Lord, inspire me to work as hard to spread respect for the sacred worth of every human being as others do in reducing man to the level of the beast.

SAME NOW AS THEN

Centuries ago the Roman Emperor Nero unleashed his soldiers on the thousands of peace-loving followers of Jesus with these words: *"Let the Christians be exterminated!"*—the same words that anti-Christians have been shouting throughout history. Nero's command was taken quite literally, as is evidenced by this report of the historian, Tacitus, writing in those days:

". . . they [the Christians] were made the subjects of sport; they were covered with the hides of wild beasts and worried to death by dogs, or nailed to crosses or set fire to, and when the day waned, burned to serve for the evening lights."

Can we, the inheritors of so glorious a tradition of martyrdom, refuse to imitate the heroic efforts of those first Christ-bearers? Can we refuse to show our faith in our God, Who Himself was crucified between two thieves?

". . . in much patience; in afflictions, in necessities, in difficulties; in blows, in prisons, in riots; in labors, in watchings, in fastings . . ." (II Corinthians 6:4–5)

᪇ Grant, O Lord, that in our love for Thee we may be ready to bear the lash of hatred and the sting of ridicule in the spirit of the martyrs of all ages.

CAN'T GET ON WITHOUT THEM

A missioner once showed a pagan Chinese woman the Ten Commandments. *"Why, these are very reasonable,"* she said, as she scanned the list, *"I don't see how anyone can very well get on without them."*

The Ten Commandments are a vital part of the foundation of our law and our way of life, yet many people have probably never seen them:

1. I am the Lord thy God; thou shalt not have strange gods before Me.
2. Thou shalt not take the name of the Lord thy God in vain.
3. Remember thou keep holy the Sabbath day.
4. Honor thy father and thy mother.
5. Thou shalt not kill.
6. Thou shalt not commit adultery.
7. Thou shalt not steal.
8. Thou shalt not bear false witness against thy neighbor.
9. Thou shalt not covet thy neighbor's wife.
10. Thou shalt not covet thy neighbor's goods.

⊷ Pray that you may be kept ever aware that true peace can be found only in the observance of His Divine Law.

REJOICE ALWAYS

Faith in God, a source of real and constant joy, is an invaluable asset to any Christopher. Religion should never be glum or gloomy, even in the midst of severe trials. Scripture is full of sound advice on this point:

1. *"A joyful mind maketh age flourishing: a sorrowful spirit drieth up the bones."* (Proverb 17:22)

2. *"Rich or poor, if his heart is good, his countenance shall be cheerful at all times."* (Ecclesiasticus 16:4)

3. *"The joyfulness of the heart is the life of a man, and a never-failing treasure of holiness: and the joy of a man is length of life. Have pity on thy own soul, pleasing God, and contain thyself: gather up thy heart in His holiness: and drive away sadness far from thee."* (Ecclesiasticus 30:23–24)

4. *"Be glad in that day and rejoice; for behold, your reward is great in heaven . . ."* (Luke 6:23)

5. *Rejoice in the Lord always; again, I say, rejoice."* (Philippians 4:4)

⋙ O God, let interior peace and joy be mine in all my works.

THE ONLY SOLUTION

A feature article in *Time* magazine on Marian Anderson, the celebrated Negro contralto, remarked that the race problem could only be *partially* explained and solved *"in political, social, and economic terms."* The problem is *"deeper than that,"* the article went on. *"Well might all Americans ponder upon the fact that it is, like all the great problems of mankind, at bottom a religious problem, and that the religious solution must be made before any other solution could be effective. It will, in fact, never be solved exclusively in human terms."*

Problems of the nation or of the world can never be solved until each of us regards them as his own. This is not only a question of recognizing our duty to our neighbor but to God as well.

"Man seeth those things that appear, but the Lord beholdeth the heart." (I Kings 16:7)

❧ Pray that the Creator of all men will give you the grace to reverence all men as His children.

HALLOWED BE THY NAME

Once, when one of Christ's disciples asked Him, "Lord, teach us to pray," Christ answered him, giving a definite form of prayer to His heavenly Father. He could have offered several suggestions, or even told the disciple to use whatever words came to his lips. Instead, He was most specific. As the gospel narrative relates it, He said:

"This, then, is to be your prayer, Our Father, who art in heaven, hallowed be Thy name;

"Thy kingdom come, Thy will be done on earth as it is in heaven;

"Give us this day our daily bread;

"And forgive us our trespasses, as we forgive them that trespass against us;

"And lead us not into temptation, but deliver us from evil. Amen." (Matthew 6: 9–13)

⋙ Lord, grant that all my prayers may be in the spirit of the prayer You gave to the world.

KEEP IT PLURAL

In praying, all of us should be especially careful to see that the words of our prayers do not become routine, that we do not pervert the meaning of the prayer for selfish personal ends.

A typical example of this kind of error is found when people pray, saying *"Our Father"* but meaning *"My Father."* Or saying *"Give us this day"* but meaning *"Give me this day."* Or *"Forgive us our trespasses"* replaced mentally by *"Forgive me . . ."* Christ did not accidentally make all the pronouns plural when He gave the prayer to His disciples as an example of how they should pray. Surely He meant for them to think of others as well as of themselves when they prayed. And the Christopher will always bear this in mind, knowing that he can do himself good only by working to better the lives of others. It is for them that he will especially pray.

"We give thanks to God always for you all; making a rememberance of you in our prayers without ceasing." (I Thessalonians 1:2)

Lord, teach me to pray for others, not merely for myself.

A SPECIAL PRICE

Several winters ago Ethel Barrymore delighted theater-goers in Franz Werfel's play *Embezzled Heaven*. Miss Barrymore's role was that of a canny Czech cook who tried to bargain her way into heaven. The amusing and ironic climax is that, just as the deal seems to fall through, she is saved because her love and sacrifice are greater than her cupidity.

Salvation cannot be bought with dollars and cents, yet we can store up treasures in heaven. All it costs us is a little time and effort.

Heaven has a price, and that price is nothing less than ourselves. We can acquire it by giving all we have to God, by devoting ourselves wholeheartedly to His Word.

"Not every man that saith to me, Lord, Lord, shall enter into the kingdom of heaven . . ." (Matthew 7:21)

⇜ Pray that you may be saved through your faith and your works.

". . . IF ONLY THERE WERE TIME"

The Metropolitan Museum of Art some time ago held a display of contemporary art at which $52,000 was awarded to American sculptors, painters, and artists in allied fields.

The award for the best painting went to the canvas of an Illinois artist. It was described as "a macabre, detailed work showing a closed door bearing a funeral wreath." Equally striking was the work's title: *"That which I should have done, I did not do."*

Few of us could win an award for painting. Many of us would not even attempt to produce a work of art. Yet there are so many things in life that we *would* do, we say, *"if only there were time."*

And so the years slip by and, with them, all our opportunities for serving others, for doing good personally to those who need help. Each day presents thousands of opportunities, large and small, for reaching out to the world as far as we can. We have only to grasp the chance. Any day is a good day to start, especially today!

"I must work the works of him that sent me, whilst it is day: the night cometh, when no man can work." (John 9:4)

◄§ Pray that you may do some good to each person you meet today.

71

EVERYBODY COUNTS

William L. Stidger, in the magazine *Your Life,* tells a story about the conductor Walter Damrosch, who once stopped his orchestra when everything was apparently going along smoothly, and asked: *"Where is the seventh flute? Where is the seventh flute?"*

As Mr. Stidger points out, the conductor didn't ask for the first flute, or the second—but the seventh. Even the seventh flute had an important place in creating the harmony the leader desired.

"We may feel inferior, untalented, not even beautiful, and some of us uneducated," Mr. Stidger comments, *"but each of us has a part to play and should play it well."*

He tells how he used to watch the man who plays the triangle in a large orchestra. Often the player would sit through the entire number, eagerly waiting. Then, toward the close, he would, with perfect timing, deftly touch the instrument and produce just the right note.

In other words, there is no really unimportant job. We should do well whatever it is our part to do.

". . . so we, though many, are one body in Christ, and, as individuals, are mutually dependent members." (Romans 12:5)

⋙ Pray that you may always be aware that the part you play in life, however small, is important.

A BETTER UNDERSTANDING

One of the most effective ways we can learn to help others is through a recognition of our own sins. We will better understand the difficulties of others when we face our own shortcomings. As the Scriptures emphasize:

1. *"All we like sheep have gone astray, every one hath turned aside into his own way: and the Lord hath laid on him the iniquity of us all."* (Isaias 53:6)

2. *"And we have gone away every man after the inclinations of his own wicked heart, to serve strange gods, and to do evil in the sight of the Lord our God."* (Baruch 1:22)

3. *"And the publican standing afar off, would not so much as lift up his eyes towards Heaven; but struck his breast, saying: O God, be merciful to me, a sinner. I say to you, this man went down into his house justified, rather than the other: because every one that exalteth himself shall be humbled; and he that humbleth himself, shall be exalted."* (Luke 18:13–14)

₰ Lord, help me to know myself better, that I may better understand others.

HERE TODAY AND GONE TOMORROW

Have you ever stopped to realize that sixty million people die each year?

Life is a constant "come and go." Each of us plays his little part. Each of us has his role assigned by God Himself.

The way *you* play *your* role, be it a leading part or insignificant, will determine the happiness of others as well as your own—for time and for eternity.

The world itself will be a little better—or a little worse—because of your "coming and going." Which will it be? You have the answer!

Play your part on the stage of life, but be careful not to lose yourself in the drama to the extent of forgetting the final curtain.

As Shakespeare said in *As You Like It:*

> "... *All the world's a stage,*
> *And all the men and women merely players:*
> *They have their exits and their entrances* ..."

"*Take ye heed, watch and pray. For ye know not when the time is.*" (Mark 13:33)

◆§ Pray that you may never fail to play your part as a Christ-bearer.

FOUR BANK BOOKS

"Miser dies on subway steps" . . . so ran a recent headline in a New York paper. Then the news item went on to tell how he was slumped on the stairs of an underground station.

Passers-by gave a hurried glance at the shabbily dressed figure apparently sleeping, then walked on incuriously.

Two hours passed before a man became interested enough to give the body a shove and discover that the man was dead. A detective searching through the dead man's pockets found no money but an identifying letter.

Going to the address, he found a dingy little flat, without light or heat, where the deceased had spent thirty years of his life. In a closet there was a box containing four bank books, representing a total savings of $9,475.

In many respects this is not an uncommon story. It shows how a misguided caution often keeps many from living a fuller, richer life, here as well as hereafter.

"But lay up to yourselves treasures in heaven . . ." (Matthew 6:20)

⏅ Lord, give me to realize that sharing with others is the secret of true happiness.

AT MY RIGHT HAND

Fifteen hundred years ago St. Patrick composed his famous prayer, "The Breastplate," which has stirred the hearts of millions ever since.

Frequent reflection on even the small excerpt given here should be of immense value to each person who strives to bring Christ into the market place:

"Christ be with me, Christ in the front,
Christ in the rear, Christ within me,
Christ below me, Christ above me,
Christ at my right hand, Christ at my left,
Christ in the fort, Christ in the chariot seat,
Christ at the helm,
Christ in the heart of every man who thinks of me,
Christ in the mouth of every man who speaks to me,
Christ in every eye that sees me,
Christ in every ear that hears me,
I bind to myself this day
The strong faith of the Invocation of the Trinity,
The faith of the Trinity in Unity.
The Creator of the Elements,
Salvation is the Lord's,
Salvation is from Christ,
Thy Salvation, O Lord, be with us forever."

NO SACRIFICE TOO GREAT

In a St. Louis foundry a stoker caught his right hand in the door of a blazing furnace. Desperately he tried to release it, knowing that if he didn't act quickly he'd be burned to death. But his efforts proved in vain.

Left with only one choice, he reached into his pocket, took out a penknife, and cut off his right hand at the wrist. He lost his hand, but he saved his life.

If a man can go to such an extreme to save his mortal life, what sacrifice is too great to make sure of eternal life?

Our Lord could not be more emphatic on this point:

"And if thy right hand is an occasion of sin to thee, cut it off, and fling it from thee: for it is better for thee that one of thy members should perish, than that thy whole body should go into Gehenna." (Matthew 5:30)

Grant that I may prepare for death, that I may fear Thy judgments, that I may escape hell, and in the end obtain heaven, through Jesus Christ our Lord.

WITHOUT FEAR

The confidence in God which is repeatedly expressed in the Old Testament should be a continuing source of inspiration for Christophers. With His help we can act fearlessly.

1. *"Although he should kill me, I will trust in him . . ."* (Job 13:15)

2. *"It is good to confide in the Lord, rather than to have confidence in man."* (Psalm 117:8)

3. *"Behold, God is my saviour, I will deal confidently, and will not fear: because the Lord is my strength, and my praise, and he is become my salvation."* (Isaias 12:2)

4. *"Blessed is the man that trusteth in the Lord, and the Lord shall be his confidence. And he shall be a tree that is planted by the waters, that spreadeth out its roots towards moisture: and it shall not fear when the heat cometh. And the leaf thereof shall be green, and in the time of drought, it shall not be solicitous, neither shall it cease at any time to bring forth fruit.* (Jeremias 17: 7-8)

Pray for an increase in confidence in God to enable you to act fearlessly, bearing all things for His sake.

SYMPATHY NOT ENOUGH

On a mountain trail in the Andes a traveler met a farmer riding on a mule, while his wife walked along behind him.

"Why isn't your wife riding?" the traveler asked the farmer.

"Because," the farmer replied, *"she has no mule."*

It is even possible, when you come to think of it, that the farmer felt sorry for his wife. He may have thought to himself, *"Too bad my wife has to walk. Now if only she had a mule! . . ."*

How often we do this! How often we fail to help those in need, out of the abundance of the things we possess, yet feel sorry for them! We express sympathy and do nothing. And all the while there lie right at hand the means whereby we could relieve their burden.

"Then He shall answer them, saying: Amen I say to you, as long as you did it not to one of these least, neither did you do it to me. And these shall go into everlasting punishment: but the just, into life everlasting." (Matthew 25: 45–46)

⋙ Grant us, O Lord, to know not only what we ought to do, but the way in which we can do it.

WHAT MOTIVE?

In La Rochefoucauld's *Maxims* there is one thought which is particularly worthy of reflection. It goes:

"However brilliant an action, it should not be esteemed great unless the result of a great motive."

Often we hear people say of someone: *"He does so much."* Yet this may not always be a compliment. While it is certain that idleness is a vice, it is not necessarily true that action is a virtue. The evil-doers of the world are frequently all too active.

The best course is always to act from a motive we can be proud of. To perform a kindness out of love—Christ-like love—is the highest behavior. Just as God so loved the world that He gave His only Begotten Son to us to purchase our salvation, so should we be inspired in all our actions by love of Him. That is the Christopher purpose. That is the Christopher motive!

"Who, when he was come and had seen the grace of God, rejoiced: and he exhorted them all with purpose of heart to continue in the Lord." (Acts 11:23)

O Lord, may I always do all things for love of Thee.

ON PRIDE

A device the Devil uses with great success when he wishes to cripple a worthy project is the stirring up of petty pride among those concerned. This is an evil which, by infecting even one or two, can nip in the bud the most promising enterprise for good.

And, with typical deception, this type of deadly pride, which aims at tripping up high-minded persons and ruining much good that could be done, persists in the name of virtue. As the poet Coleridge well said:

"And the Devil did grin, for his darling sin
Is pride that apes humility."

Since this treacherous vice so often appears in harmless garb and manifests itself in so many disguises, we should be especially alert to see that we do not succumb to it ourselves.

We can better avoid the pitfalls of pride by concentrating our minds and hearts on the practice of *true* humility which is rooted in the knowledge that all we are and all we have comes from God.

". . . without Me you can do nothing." (John 15:5)

Pray that you may be ever conscious that without the aid of God you can achieve nothing.

THE PROBLEM REMAINS

When the Duke of Windsor was Prince of Wales he once visited, in the same afternoon, the newly-built steamship *Queen Mary* and some Glasgow slums. Afterward he said to a friend: *"How do you reconcile a world that has produced that mighty ship with the slums we have just visited?"*

A British scientist, after hearing this remark, observed: *"That is the problem that we have to solve, and it is useless to go out and solve scientific problems if you cannot solve that."*

In our pride in technological advances we must not forget that there are many who are in misery the world over. The invention of a new kind of washing machine means little to the man who has no clothes. If we are enjoying a life of comforts, we should be particularly solicitous about others, making sure that we are not forgetting our responsibilities toward our neighbors.

"Bear ye one another's burdens; and so you shall fulfill the law of Christ." (Galatians 6:2)

⊷ Lord, teach me to remember those who suffer privation.

YOU CAN'T WIN

An English comedian recently wrote in the London *Daily Sketch* the following analysis of the money problem:

"If a man runs after money, he's money mad;
If he keeps it, he's a capitalist;
If he spends it, he's a playboy;
If he doesn't get it, he lacks ambition.
If he gets it without working for it, he's a parasite;
And if he accumulates it after a lifetime of hard work,
People call him a fool who never got anything out of life."

It is true that people say all these things. In fact, when you think about it, you'll find that almost anybody can be criticized for *anything*.

The cure? Only this: make sure which is the right course, *then follow it, without bothering about what others may say*. If you are in the right, their criticism should only be a further incentive.

"Blessed are ye when they shall revile you, and persecute you, and speak all that is evil against you, untruly for my sake." (Matthew 5:11)

꙳ Lord, let me be honest in my judgment of myself, valuing the opinions of others at their true worth.

PEOPLE ARE MIRRORS

A psychologist once asked a group of college students to jot down, in thirty seconds, the initials of the people they disliked. Some of the students taking the test could think of only one person. Others listed as many as fourteen.

But the interesting fact that came out of this bit of research was this: *those who disliked the largest number were themselves the most widely disliked.*

When we find ourselves continually disliking others, we ought to bring ourselves up short and ask *ourselves* the question: *"What is wrong with me?"*

Very likely if we develop an aversion to those around us, it is not because they deserve our antipathy, but because *we* are lacking in some particular quality we profess to see missing in *them*. Other people are mirrors, in the sense that what we see in them is a reflection of ourselves.

"A man has no enemy worse than himself." (Cicero)

✍ Lord, help us to meet criticism—not by self-defense, but by self-examination.

MORE THAN KNOWLEDGE

One day when Thomas Aquinas was preaching to the local populace on the love of God, he saw an old woman listening attentively to his every word. And inspired by her eagerness to learn more about her God whom she loved so dearly, he said to the people:

It is better to be this unlearned woman, loving God with all her heart, than the most learned theologian lacking love.

A great theologian himself, Thomas Aquinas knew that our main avenue of approach to God is love. Though he never belittled knowledge of God—indeed, he wrote volumes monumental in their deep knowledge of the things of God—he insisted on this cardinal point, that if we do not love God and His creatures, our neighbors, and work to increase that love, it matters little how much we know about Him.

"Christianity taught man that love is worth more than intelligence."—Jacques Maritain

⇜ Jesus, Redeemer who died for me, give me the love to live for Thee.

STANDING STILL IN A HURRY

Some time ago we heard a strange story. The pilot of a small transport plane said that he had been caught in a one hundred and fifty-mile gale, which held his plane perfectly still. The motors were roaring, he claimed, but the plane was not moving an inch.

"*It was weird,*" he concluded, "*to be going one hundred and fifty miles an hour and yet not be going anywhere at all!*"

Sometimes we seem to be doing something very much like this. No matter how hard we push forward, we seem to be getting nowhere at all. Then is the time for us to remember that he who does not try to go ahead is bound to find that he is going back. *If the pilot of the plane had shut off his motors, he would probably never have lived to tell the story.* It was only because he made every effort to go forward that he was even able to stand still!

"*Not to progress is to go back.*"—Latin proverb

✑ Keep us ever aware, O Lord, that not to go forward in Thy name is to go back; that not to reach out, continually, with Thy love to others, is to weaken our love of Thee.

NO EXCUSE

Johnny was a little boy quick with excuses. One morning when he came to school unprepared the teacher asked wearily: *"Well, John, where is your exercise this morning?"*

"Well, sir, you said yesterday we were to do lesson seventeen."

"Yes?"

"Then last night Jimmy told me it was number eighteen we were supposed to do."

"But you didn't bring in any," the teacher pointed out.

"Well, I was afraid to do the wrong one."

When we don't want to do a thing, we seldom have difficulty finding an excuse, often a very plausible one. But merely having a good excuse does not mean we can neglect duties which are ours.

"And they began all at once to make excuse. The first said to him: I have bought a farm, and I must needs go out and see it: I pray thee, hold me excused." (Luke 14:18)

⋙ Pray that you may always serve with good works, instead of serving up good excuses.

WORDS ARE NOT ENOUGH

In 1915 the Congressional Commission on Industrial Relations issued its final report after listening to the opinions of more than two hundred employers' representatives who provided a good cross section of business thought in those days.

One of the most significant results of the investigation was this: while not one of the businessmen who testified found fault with the workingman for wanting better working conditions and a higher standard of living, few were willing to take a single step to bring about these improved conditions.

So long as they could remain on the level of *verbal* recognition of the rights and needs of others, they found it easy to admit something *ought* to be done. But when practical solutions were presented, they backed out. Yet if only they had translated their beliefs into concrete deeds then, we might have much less to worry about today.

"For us, Communism has a particular significance. It is evidence of our unfulfilled duty." (Jules Saliege, Archbishop of Toulouse)

வ§ Help us, O Lord, to show our love of Your image in our fellow men, not only in our words but in our works.

A GOOD BET

The gatekeeper at a famous race track took $1200—his life savings—out of the bank and gave it to his nephew to help the boy pay his way through college.

When asked how he could afford the gesture, the old man smiled. *"Day in and day out I watch thousands of men bet on horses and lose their shirts. The way I figure it, a man might stand a chance to make a killing if he bets on a human being."*

Betting on our fellow man is a sure thing. We can't possibly lose because, if all else fails, our good deed itself pays us back, giving us the satisfaction of having done something worth while, storing up treasures in heaven.

"Turn not away thy face from thy neighbor . . ."
(Ecclesiasticus 41:26)

✒ Pray that whatever it be, to whomever it be, it be done for God's sake.

WHY NOT TELL HER?

We met a girl a while ago who had only one complaint to make against her husband. Seen in the perspective of a lifetime, perhaps it isn't an important one, but small things sometimes loom large in their everyday context.

"My husband always praises me to other people," she said. *"Constantly I hear from friends the wonderful things he has said about me. But I miss something, because he never gets around to saying these same things to me, to my face."*

This complaint, however trivial it may seem, shows something about our daily life. We all tend to let those we love take our love for granted. We forget that everyone has a need to be assured that he is loved.

"Let your love be free from hypocrisy." (Romans 12:9)

◈§ Lord, teach me to praise others sincerely and without flattery.

NO TIME TO LOSE

The ship's chief engineer, coming down the companionway into the engine room, shouted: *"How long have you been working in this compartment?"*

The fireman, recently assigned to the crew, answered honestly: *"Ever since I saw you coming down the ladder."*

There is a constant temptation for all of us to *"take it easy"* until an emergency arises.

Often we tend to excuse our own spiritual idleness, putting off action to some future time which we imagine will be more opportune.

We are naturally inclined to believe that a kind of routine goodness is enough, and we postpone any really energetic spiritual activity. In actuality *every* day is the *right* day for spiritual labor—is the proper time for directing our moral energies toward our eternal goal. Indeed, there is no time to lose!

"Behold, now is the acceptable time; behold now is the day of salvation. (II Corinthians 6:2)

◦§ Pray that you may ever be alert in serving Christ and the common good.

A DOUBLE EFFECT

Each year Americans spend millions of dollars in desperate attempts to lose weight, while still continuing to eat their three full meals a day.

There is an irresistible lure in a full-page advertisement like the one that appeared in a Chicago daily. It said in part:

"New easy way to take off pounds and inches . . . without starving . . . without exercise . . . start losing fat the first day . . ."

It would be far cheaper, as well as more effective and more profitable both for body and soul, to follow the age-old program of just plain fasting. In the words of the New Testament: *"Repent, for the Kingdom of Heaven is at hand."* (Matthew 3:2)

❧ Pray, that as you persevere in fasting throughout this season, so you may persevere in devotion to Him throughout your life.

ADVERSITY DOESN'T KILL

Three hundred years ago a prisoner condemned to the Tower of London carved on the wall of his cell this sentiment to keep up his spirits during his long imprisonment:

"It is not adversity that kills, but the impatience with which we bear adversity."

Rebelling against difficulties or obstacles that cannot legitimately be avoided only makes a bad situation worse. Ordinary common sense recommends that we ride the storm, not buck it. But going one step further—going from the natural to the supernatural—makes it easier still to bear adversity patiently.

Once you recognize that your suffering can actually bear fruit if you try to have the same purpose as Christ, then there will be the hidden joy of accomplishment even in bearing the Cross which He bore for us nineteen hundred years ago.

". . . In thy sorrow endure, and in thy humiliation keep patience." (Ecclesiasticus 2:4)

≈§ O Lord, give me the grace to bear patiently what must be borne, for Thy sake.

THE COURAGE TO SAY "NO"

Many observers fear that the self-indulgence and moral indifference spreading over the world may destroy freedom. Walter Lippmann put it this way:

"Without order or authority in the spirit of man the free way of life leads through weakness, disorganization, self-indulgence, and moral indifference to the destruction of freedom itself. The tragic ordeal through which the Western world is passing was prepared in the long period of easy liberty, during which men . . . forgot that their freedom was achieved by heroic sacrifice . . . They forgot that their rights were founded on their duties . . . they thought it clever to be cynical and enlightened to be unbelieving, and sensible to be soft."

Most of us know we must bring forth fruit worthy of penance; that with God's help we must be firm when tempted to be weak; that we must have the courage to say, "No" when it would be easy to say "Yes." Knowing this, we ought—if we wish to preserve our sacred freedom— to help bring order and discipline into the main stream of life.

"Bring forth therefore fruit worthy of penance." (Matthew 3:8)

⊷ Pray that you use the talents God has given you to preserve our precious heritage of freedom.

LET'S DO IT NOW

Always popular are the following words, which are attributed to Stephen Grellet, French-born Quaker who died in New Jersey in 1855. For all of us Grellet's simple yet charged remarks can be a source of inspiration:

"I shall pass through this world but once. Any good thing I can do, or any kindness that I can show any human being, let me do it now and not defer it. For I shall not pass this way again."

How true these words are! And since we have but one brief "testing period" here in which to prepare for eternity, it behooves us not to waste or misuse it. The chance, once gone, will never be offered to us again.

"Love not the world, nor the things which are in the world. If any man love the world, the charity of the Father is not in him . . . And the world passeth away, and the concupiscence thereof: but he that doth the will of God abideth forever." (I John 2:15, 17)

◆§ Lord, teach me to live in the world, not being of the world, and teach me to do good, thus storing up treasures in Heaven.

HOLY THURSDAY

This day, sacred to every follower of Christ, commemorates the Last Supper, the institution of the Holy Eucharist, the Sacrifice of the Altar which, St. Paul reminds us, is a *"memorial of the death of Christ."* Here, in the words of Paul to the Corinthians, is the simple yet significant story of the first Holy Thursday:

". . . the Lord Jesus, on the night in which he was betrayed, took bread, and giving thanks broke, and said, 'This is my body which shall be given up for you; do this in remembrance of me.' In like manner also the cup, after he had supped, saying, 'This cup is the new covenant in my blood; do this as often as you drink it, in remembrance of me. For as often as you shall eat this bread and drink the cup, you proclaim the death of the Lord, until he comes." (I Corinthians 11:23–26)

❧ Pray that you may seek out the God of us all and from Him take your strength.

GOOD FRIDAY

This is a day of failure—but failure only from a *human point of view*. It is the failure of the few years of life that precede the triumph which will last for eternity. For every true Christopher, Good Friday should be a pointed reminder that being a Christ-bearer also means being a *cross-bearer*. Christ Himself could not have put it more specifically: *"And he said to all: If any man will come after me, let him deny himself and take up his cross daily and follow me."* (Luke 9:23)

Christ doesn't force us one inch. He leaves things entirely in our own hands. But if we—*of our own free will*—decide to carry Christ into the market place, we must not merely be *ready* for endless trials and tribulations. It is our business to go out and *meet* them. Again, as Christ pointed out: *"He that taketh not up his cross, and followeth me is not worthy of me."* (Matthew 10:38)

With each of us the failure of the cross must go before the final triumph. We must be willing to fail and fail again—*even to be crucified*—in order to play our part in saving the world.

≈§ Teach me, O Jesus Crucified, to take up my cross each day cheerfully and without hesitation.

HOLY SATURDAY

Jesus is dead. He lies in the tomb. He died that you might live, proving His love for you to the last drop of His blood.

His request to you is to continue what He began. He died for all. He wishes to continue to live here in the souls of men and to carry on His work through *your* co-operation.

In His first appearance to His disciples after the Resurrection, Christ uttered these thrilling words, giving His followers the sublime mission of bringing peace to the world: *"Peace be to you. As the Father hath sent me, I also send you."* (John 20:19)

This was more than just a polite suggestion. It was a solemn command to carry the peace of God to all mankind—that precious peace for which all mankind longs. No greater support has been given any mission. The whole of heaven is behind anyone who throws himself into the task . . . That is a direct invitation and challenge to *you*.

"Yet so, if we suffer with him, that we may also be glorified with him." (Romans 8:17)

❧ Pray that you may do your part in carrying Christ's peace to all men.

EASTER SUNDAY

Gaily-dressed crowds will stroll up and down Fifth Avenue today in the annual Easter parade. Millions of people who ordinarily stay away from church will attend services. This is a good sign, a heartening one. The majority of people still have a reverence for God—even though they may show it by public worship only infrequently, or not at all.

It is this group that particularly need the attention you as a Christopher can give them. In a friendly way, you can do something to bring Christ to them and them to Christ.

In a vague way, at least, most people know the meaning of Easter. You can, by work and prayer, make it more real for them. You can help them understand that their sorrows, sufferings, and defeats can be turned into triumphant joy when united to the suffering of Christ.

"... *Christ rising again from the dead, dieth now no more, death shall have no dominion over him.*" (Romans 6:9)

❧ Pray that the millions who are indifferent to God may be brought back to Him.

HOLD FAST

Much attention is given to the wills of prominent people, to the distribution of their wealth and property. But one of the most meaningful testaments we know of is that of a New York woman who left her children a valuable piece of advice in addition to her worldly goods. These are the last lines of her will:

"Love one another. Hold fast to that whether you understand one another or not, and remember nothing really matters except being kind to one another in the name of Christ and to all the world as far as you can reach."

"Hold fast" . . . it is interesting to note the woman's choice of words. She knew well that it wasn't an easy task she had bequeathed her heirs. And yet, she told her children not only to be kind to one another but to *"all the world as far as you can reach."* This farsighted woman certainly practiced the second great commandment:

"And the second is like to this: Thou shalt love thy neighbour as thyself." (Matthew 22:39)

✍ Help us, O Lord, to hold fast to our aim to bring the love of Christ to all, as far as we can reach.

FINAL TRIUMPH

Sometimes when it seems to us that the wrong side is winning, it is comforting to remember that the final Judge of all is ever mindful of those who are loyal to Him in fair weather and foul.

1. *"For I know that my Redeemer liveth, and in the last day I shall rise out of the earth. And I shall be clothed again with my skin, and in my flesh I shall see my God. Whom I myself shall see, and my eyes shall behold, and not another: this my hope is laid up in my bosom."* (Job 19:25–27)

2. *"But the souls of the just are in the hand of God, and the torment of death shall not touch them. In the sight of the unwise they seemed to die: and their departure was taken for misery: And their going away from us, for utter destruction: but they are in peace."* (Wisdom 3:1–3)

3. *"But the just shall live for evermore: and their reward is with the Lord, and the care of them with the most High. Therefore shall they receive a kingdom of glory, and a crown of beauty at the hand of the Lord . . ."* (Wisdom 5:16–17)

☙ Pray that you always keep your mind and heart focused on your eternal destiny.

A VICIOUS CYCLE

There is an old saying that goes:
"Peace begets prosperity;
Prosperity begets pride;
Pride begets prejudice;
Prejudice begets war;
War begets poverty."

The thoughts expressed here may be an over-simplification of specific problems. Yet one transition—that of *prosperity* to *pride*—seems especially insidious. Prosperity should offer us opportunities to extend our interest in others. Yet, paradoxically, prosperity often begets *self-interest*—a desire to advance our own welfare, oblivious of our relationship to others.

Christ's balance wheel is safe and sane: *"Love thy neighbor as thyself."* We are expected to take care of ourselves, of course. But that doesn't mean we should spend 98 per cent of our thought and time on ourselves, especially when He favors us with prosperity. When we do, the trouble begins: *"Pride begets prejudice; prejudice begets war; war begets poverty."*

"Whenever a man desires a thing inordinately, he becomes restless. A proud and avaricious man is never at rest; a poor and humble man abides always in the fullness of peace." (Imitation of Christ 1:6, 1–2)

✑ Help us, O Lord, in our prosperity to remember the adversities of others.

SOMETHING MISSING

Great is the temptation to think that because we possess the Truth we need nothing further. We fulfil our faith only when we put the Truth to work. Something vital will be missing until we make the Truth we possess a living reality, until we reach out with it to all men as far as we can.

"What shall it profit, my brethren, if a man say he hath faith but hath not works? Shall faith be able to save him?

"So faith also, if it have not works, is dead in itself . . .

"But wilt thou know, O vain man, that faith without works is dead?

"Do you see that by works a man is justified; and not by faith only?

"For even as the body without the spirit is dead, so also faith without works is dead." (James 2:14, 17, 20, 24, 26)

⋙ Pray for that faith which will move mountains, and then implement that faith with your own good deeds.

CAUGHT NAPPING

A woman in Washington, D.C., sold her house, put the cash in her purse, and set out across the country, bound for Honolulu. In San Francisco she decided to sit up all night in the waiting room of a railroad station, afraid she might lose the money if she went to sleep in a hotel. But she was unable to keep awake, and toward dawn she dozed off for a few minutes. When she woke, the purse was gone and with it her steamship ticket and $5,435—all she had in the world.

We go to great pains to protect our material possessions, but our spiritual treasure is frequently neglected. Once we realize how valuable this treasure is for all eternity, we will exercise even greater care in protecting it than we show for our earthly goods. We will never let ourselves be caught napping. Always we will be vigilant.

"But this know ye, that if the householder did know at what hour the thief would come, he would surely watch, and would not suffer his house to be broken open." (Luke 12:39)

O God, grant that I may be ever concerned about the things of eternity and never tire in my awareness of everlasting Truth.

ONCE WE WAKE UP

At the end of World War I there was a loud cry that Christianity had failed. Promptly G. K. Chesterton, the great English writer, took those who held this view to task. *"The trouble with Christianity is, not that it's failed,"* he said, *"but that it's never been tried . . . not that it can't remake the world, but that it's difficult."*

If everyone who has the privilege of Christian training and the grace to adhere to it were to make use of Christ's principles in every walk of life, we should soon see Christianity changing the face of the globe. The Devil, knowing this, keeps alive the fiction that it is impossible to bring high ideals into the workaday world, and the enemies of Christ make it their business always to proclaim that Christianity won't work.

Yet, despite this, the one thing that terrifies the godless the world over is the fear that some day those who believe in Christ will wake up—and start acting their beliefs. Once that happens, most of the great problems which plague mankind will disappear overnight.

". . . because we hope in the living God, Who is the Saviour of all men . . ." (I Timothy 4:10)

❧ Pray for the strength and courage to make the salvation of the world *your* concern.

DOUBTING THOMAS

It happened that Thomas, one of the twelve apostles, who is called Didymus, was not with the rest when Jesus first appeared to them after the Resurrection. When he finally did join them, they said to him: *"We have seen the Lord."* But he said to them: *"Except I shall see in his hands the print of the nails, and put my finger into the place of the nails, and put my hand into his side, I will not believe."*

And after eight days again His disciples were within, and Thomas with them. Jesus cometh, the doors being shut, and stood in the midst, and said: *"Peace be to you."*

Then he saith to Thomas: *"Put in thy finger hither, and see my hands; and bring hither thy hand, and put it into my side; and be not faithless, but believing."*

Thomas answered, and said to him: *"My Lord, and my God."*

Jesus saith to him: *"Because thou hast seen me, Thomas, thou hast believed: blessed are they that have not seen, and have believed."* (John 20:25–29)

⇦ Lord, increase my belief in Thee.

PERVERTED TALENT

One of Hitler's most surprising statements is a remark he made in 1939, just before the war.

"All my life," he said, *"I have wanted to be a great painter in oils. . . . As soon as I have carried out my program for Germany, I shall take up my painting. I feel that I have it in my soul to become one of the great artists of the age and that future historians will remember me not for what I have done for Germany, but for my art."*

We seldom think of Hitler as a frustrated artist. But he wasn't the only one among the prominent Nazis so inclined. Goebbels was an obscure poet in his youth; Funk was a musician; Baldur von Schirach wrote verse, and Rosenberg dabbled in architecture.

We have a tendency to admire "imagination" and "sensitivity" as if they were positive virtues, yet it was precisely the perverted imagination of the Nazis that made their cruelty more horrible. Like any talent or trait God gives us, imagination and sensitivity must be put to work for a good cause, devoted to bettering this life, not destroying it.

᷿ Pray that all art will be used for the glory of God.

"WE BELONG TO THE WORLD"

A former English Communist, recently returned from China, told of her experiences there and mentioned in particular what she had observed at a mission hospital run by a group of nursing Sisters. *"What I saw was hard to believe,"* she confided to a gathering of Protestant women at the Hotel Commodore in New York. *"There was scarcely a square foot in the whole place not covered by some poor Chinese, sick or wounded. Yet nobody was turned away . . . some spot was found for everyone. And what care they got! Every person was treated with a tender and tireless solicitude I have seldom seen.*

"The Sisters in charge of the hospital obviously were Europeans, but from what country I wasn't sure. So I asked the Sister Superior: 'Sister, to what country do you and the other nuns belong?' Without a moment's hesitation she replied in words I'll never forget: 'We belong to no country. We belong to the world. We are sisters in Christ. We are sisters of all men!'

"Until we can echo the conviction of that Sister, until we can say that we are sisters and brothers in Christ to all men, the world will never know a real and lasting peace," were the closing words of this ex-Communist.

❧ Help us to remember, O Lord, that we belong to the world because we belong to Thee.

FROM A BEAUTY PARLOR

A young lady who works in a Chicago beauty parlor carries on a far-reaching apostolate in a quiet but most effective way. While massaging the well-fed bodies of women who enjoy eating yet want to avoid showing the results, she makes it her business to say a fervent prayer for their souls. She prays that each of them may show as much interest in her *spiritual well-being* as she does in the *physical* side of her life.

In addition, she places each tip given her in a small box, and at regular intervals sends the accumulation to a missioner in China who cares for six hundred lepers. She feels she should be instrumental in seeing that this money from those who are blessed with the best of life's goods is transmitted to those who are suffering from one of the worst of physical afflictions.

No matter how insignificant our position in life may be, we can still be Christophers—can still do something to reach the world—by prayer and by work; we can make the world a bit the better for our being in it.

"Or know you not, that your members are the temple of the Holy Ghost, who is in you, whom you have from God; and you are not your own?" (I Corinthians 6:19)

⊷ Pray earnestly that your minds and bodies may truly become temples of the Holy Spirit.

TIME CANNOT DESTROY

When Daniel Webster, the great statesman and orator, spoke at Faneuil Hall, Boston, in 1852, he underlined the great service anyone renders who dedicates himself to teaching God's truth:

"If we work upon marble, it will perish.
If we work upon brass, time will efface it.
If we rear temples, they will crumble to dust.
But if we work upon men's immortal minds,
If we imbue them with high principles,
With the just fear of God and love of their fellow man,
We engrave on those tablets something which no time
can efface,
And which will brighten and brighten to all eternity."

Those who take up a career in teaching, with a sense of devotion and dedication that makes seemingly great difficulties become very small indeed, clearly recognize the privilege of being God's instruments in bringing His Truth even to the least of men. For them, *purpose makes the difference!*

O Lord, send teachers, sworn to Thy Truth, into every classroom in our land and over the world.

THE SPHERES THAT COUNT

If you stop and reflect for a moment you will probably agree that the great majority of the best citizens in every community, rich or poor, educated or uneducated, are engaged in professions or pursuits that have little purpose beyond earning a living. Too seldom are they found in occupations that are concerned with the formation of thought or the leadership of people. In more instances than not they are merchants or elevator operators, manufacturers or druggists, bakers or doctors, barbers or railroad executives.

What a refreshing change for the better will come once enough people with high purpose *also* make it their business to go as Christophers into the fields of education, government, writing, trade unions, social service, and libraries. Once they bring to bear their tremendous influence over the minds and hearts of men more persons will strive to take an active Christopher role themselves in these same influential spheres.

"And he said to them: Go you also into my vineyard . . ." (Matthew 20:4)

⋘ Lord, let me use my talents to help others gain eternal life.

THE POWER OF THE PRESS

"I think we'll have a good potato crop this year," a newspaper editor told his housekeeper one morning.

"No such thing," asserted the housekeeper. *"I think the crop will be poor."*

Ignoring her remark, the editor proceeded to his office and caused to be inserted in the evening paper *his* estimate of the crop situation.

That night when he returned home he found the housekeeper waiting for him with a sheepish grin on her face and a copy of the paper in her hand. *"I was wrong,"* she said apologetically. *"It says right here in the paper that the crop will be excellent this fall."*

It's human nature to believe more readily what one sees in print than what one learns by word of mouth. All of us tend to read too uncritically. Playing this for all it is worth, those out to wreck the country strive to get jobs in the field of writing—jobs that count. The solution? To get thousands of Christophers, possessed of the same zeal and daring, to outwrite the enemies of our way of life: to match them word for word, paragraph for paragraph, truth for error.

"And the Lord said to me: Take thee a great book and write in it with a man's pen. . . ." (Isaias 8:1)

Pray that God will send thousands of Christ-bearers, possessed of zeal and daring, into the field of writing to outwrite those who hate Him.

REACHING THE YOUNG

In every country it is the same. Promoters of subversion *always* make it their business to situate themselves where they can reach the *many*, not the *few*. The Nazis were shrewd enough to see this, so they encouraged every follower possible to go into teaching. It was their one fixed idea to condition German youth to believe that they were *animals*—nothing more.

The results speak for themselves. After twelve years of such teaching, millions of young Germans—basically no different from Americans of like age—actually began to *act* like animals.

Yet all during that period too many good German people had retired into their own little worlds, *taking care of themselves,* often unaware that those with evil ideas were *taking care of everyone else!* . . . Such was the pattern then laid out for today's subversives.

The same thing can happen here. Especially if those who know the Truth, who are aware of the sacredness of the individual, do not take the trouble to share their own beliefs with the rising generation.

•§ Pray for the countless millions over the earth who are still being taught that they are nothing more than animals.

NOTE THE EMPHASIS

Repeatedly Our Lord stressed that we should do *first* what most of us by Nature are inclined to do *last*. He didn't say: *"Love thyself and then, if it isn't too much bother, love others."* Most emphatically, He put it just the other way: *"Love thy neighbor as thyself."*

He could have urged us to be *"simple as doves and wise as serpents."* Instead, He said: *"Be ye wise as serpents and simple as doves."* Most good people now are "simple as doves"—which requires little effort—whereas most of those bent on evil are "wise as serpents." Once there are enough followers of Christ who combine both qualities in the proper order, then great things are bound to happen.

Again, Christ did *not* say: *We should go into the byways and the highways.* He purposely put the more important *first*: *Going into the highways and the byways.* Christians at present are largely confining themselves to the "byways." Those striving relentlessly to destroy the world and enslave mankind concentrate almost entirely on the "highways," knowing that once they control the main spheres of influence (education, government, labor-management, writing, et cetera) they automatically control the "byways" as well.

⋙ Pray that a million Christophers will match the daring enterprise of the godless and go into the "highways" as well as the "byways"—and thus win the world back to Christ!

"AS GOOD AS THAT"

During a heavy storm at sea a nervous woman passenger on a large liner went to the captain, seeking reassurance. *"Captain,"* she asked tremulously, *"are we in great danger?"*

"Don't worry, madam," he answered, *"after all, we are in the hands of God."*

"Oh," she gasped, terror written on her face, *"is it as bad as that?"*

We are always in the hands of God, whether or not the weather is stormy. *It is as good as that!* Sometimes we forget God's presence until the last moment, until we feel the storm around us. We should be aware, even during the calm, of the buoying support of Christ.

"And they came to him, and awaked him, saying: Lord, save us, we perish. And Jesus saith to them: Why are you fearful, O ye of little faith? Then rising up he commanded the winds, and the sea, and there came a great calm." (Matthew 8:25–26)

❧ In Thee, O Lord, I place all my hope and trust.

HARDER HERE—EASIER THERE

Several years ago an elderly lady made a generous gift to the poor. When asked if she could really afford it, her answer was memorable.

"I'm seventy-four now," she said. *"My husband—God rest his soul!—died twenty-three years ago. He wasn't able to leave me much money, so for all this time I've earned a living by scrubbing and washing. But I felt I should do more than that. I wanted to help those worse off than I am. God has been good to me. I have my health, a roof over my head, enough to eat. So many people don't have these blessings. And then I thought it would be better to work a little bit harder in this life and take my rest in the life to come."*

It's interesting to notice that those who take things *"a little bit harder in this life"* often seem to have a foretaste of heaven here below, while those who seek heaven on earth through self-gratification know only bitter failure.

"If we would do only a little violence to ourselves in the beginning, we would afterwards be able to do all things with ease and joy." (Imitation of Christ 1:11, 18)

◄§ Lord, help me to choose the harder path that leads to Thee.

NO FAILURE

Judged by ordinary standards, the life of Francis Thompson, the nineteenth-century English poet, was a miserable failure. He failed successively as a student, a book agent, a shoemaker's apprentice, and a soldier. At twenty-one he was a drug addict, prematurely aged, sleeping on park benches and writing poems on wrapping paper, making his living by running errands and selling matches.

Then he was discovered by an editor, Wilfrid Meynell, and his wife Alice, herself a poet. Thompson went to live with them, and stayed with them for years, until he died. He devoted himself wholeheartedly to his writings, and his talent was recognized. Of his works, one, his great religious poem—*The Hound of Heaven*—won a place for itself among the most celebrated minor poems in our language.

Success is something we must find in our own way by co-operating with God. Poverty and hunger and neglect do not necessarily mean failure, though they are often mistaken for it. We fail only when we give ourselves up for lost, refusing the helping hand of others, persisting in despair.

"All things betray thee, who betrayest Me." (*The Hound of Heaven*)

◄§ Grant, Lord, that I may see that life holds no failure like the failure to hope in Thee.

TWO POWERS

Deserted by his armies and imprisoned on the island of St. Helena, Napoleon wrote in a letter to a friend the following impressive words:

"There are in the world two powers—the sword and the spirit. The spirit has always vanquished the sword."

A powerful thought—from such a spokesman. Napoleon well knew the futility of earthly success, the shifting sands of temporal power and material dominion.

The spirit can vanquish not only the sword, but all enemies. Usually the battleground is within *us*, and we must decide with which opponent we will side. It isn't hard to pick the winner.

"For what doth it profit a man, if he gain the whole world, and suffer the loss of his own soul? Or what exchange shall a man give for his soul?" (Matthew 16:26)

⫷ Help me, O Lord, to remember nothing is worth the loss of my soul.

OPEN FROM WITHIN

In Holman Hunt's painting, "The Light of the World," Christ is shown in a garden at midnight, holding a lantern in His left hand. With His right hand He is knocking on a heavily paneled door.

When the painting was unveiled, a critic remarked to the painter, *"Mr. Hunt, the work is unfinished. There is no handle on the door."*

"That," Hunt answered, *"is the door to the human heart. It can be opened only from the inside."*

God does not force Himself or His law upon us; we are free to deny Him. But we are reminded constantly of God's love and desire to come to us.

It is most important for all Christophers to follow this same respectful approach in reaching others. Be ever ready to share Christ's truth, but gently offer it to others. You can't force it on them.

"Behold, I stand at the gate and knock. If any man shall hear my voice and open to me the door, I will come in to him. . . ." (Apocalypse 3:20)

❧ Pray that you may always be persuasive, not belligerent, in bringing the truth to others.

"DO NOT THOU FORGET"

As we were sitting in the office of a busy college president one day, our eye was caught by a little framed plaque with an interesting saying on it. It was almost hidden behind a row of books, so as to be invisible to the casual visitor but constantly in the view of the man behind the desk.

Here are the words that this president made it a point to keep before him all through his day's work. The plaque read: *"LORD, I SHALL BE VERIE BUSIE THIS DAY. I MAY FORGET THEE, BUT DO NOT THOU FORGET ME."* These are the words of Sir Jacob Astley's memorable prayer before the battle of Newbury.

This simple thought suggests an important principle: by directing our "intention" we can make our every act a prayer. Thus our daily tasks are made more meaningful and more rewarding as well.

"All whatsoever you do in word or in work, do all in the name of the Lord Jesus Christ, giving thanks to God and the Father by him." (Colossians 3:17)

≈§ Lord, help me to make my every act a prayer.

MAY DAY—LOYALTY DAY

For centuries May 1 has been observed as Our Lady's Day. But more recently it has become a rallying day all over the world for the enemies of Christ. In order to restore a spiritual note to May Day, the Christophers, for the past several years, have encouraged millions to set aside May 1 as a day of prayer for the vast section of humanity now dominated by the opponents of Christ, and also for those misguided souls who persist in spreading a hatred of God and man.

May Day may also serve as an occasion for nationwide public demonstrations of loyalty to the spiritual foundation of our country. Patriotic organizations would do well to hold public gatherings or parades—not to demonstrate *against* anybody or anything, but rather to demonstrate *for* the basic spiritual truth on which our nation is founded. As the President said at his Inaugural last year: *"We believe that all men are created equal because they are created in the image of God. From this faith we will not be moved."*

Say frequently during the day this prayer: "Saviour of the world, save Russia."

THE BLIND SEE

Two blind beggars on a busy Midwestern street were soliciting alms from the hurrying passers-by. Both were pitiful figures, yet one of them, strangely enough, seemed to be having much more success than the other. The nickels and dimes poured into his cup, while people walked past the first beggar with hardly a glance. An interested observer of the scene finally discovered the reason. Instead of the usual card reading, *"I am Blind,"* the successful mendicant's card read: *"It is May and I am Blind."*

He attracted the attention of the passers-by with this reminder of the beauty of a spring he could not see— a beauty that perhaps he feared they were missing. Deprived of sight, he could understand how much of the world goes unseen by almost everyone. Many of us live with a blindness that is not physical, unaware of the grandeur of the Creator's bounty in the world that lies around us.

". . . seeing they see not, and hearing they hear not, neither do they understand." (Matthew 13:13)

⧫ Pray for the grace to persevere in helping those who cannot see the Light of His Truth.

THE BASIS OF HARMONY

When he was conductor of the New York Philharmonic Orchestra, Artur Rodzinski said: *"In our orchestra we have many nationalities, types, and temperaments. We have learned to forget individual likes, dislikes, and differences of temperament for the sake of music to which we have dedicated our lives. I often wonder if we could not solve the world's problems on a similar basis of harmony.*

"Think what a single individual in a symphony orchestra can accomplish," the famous maestro continued, *"by giving up his individual traits and ambitions in the service of music . . . Suppose that in life you had the same all-embracing love for the whole of mankind and for your neighbor in particular. Only when every one of us and every nation learns the secret of love for all mankind will the world become a great orchestra, following the beat of the Greatest Conductor of all."*

Not until all men look up to the "Greatest Conductor of all," giving Him their devotion and wholehearted love, will they learn the "secret of love for all mankind."

"For you have put off the old manhood with its practices, and have put on the new, which is being renewed unto fuller knowledge according to the Image of its Creator. In it there is not Greek and Jew, circumcision and uncircumcision, foreigner, Scythian, slave and freeman, but Christ is all and in all." (Colossians 3:9–11)

❧ O God, grant that I may be an effective instrument in teaching that there can be no true brotherhood of man without recognition of Thee as Father of all.

CHARACTERISTICS OF A CHRISTOPHER (A)

A Christopher may be distinguished by several characteristics. First of all:

By love for all people. Most of us love "some of the people some of the time," but few of us love "all of the people all of the time." A dangerous trend is developing among Christians. They are beginning to hate, to return hatred for hatred. This method has never yet had lasting results with Christians or anti-Christians. Love, on the other hand, has made possible the very condition of Christian civilization that protects every individual from the evils that follow in the wake of hatred. We must remember that Christ died for *all* men, even those who crucified Him. He asked us to bring His love to "all men" of "all nations." Upon this basic principle rests the whole spirit of the Christopher.

"By this shall all men know that you are my disciples, if you have love for one another." (John 13:35)

⋙ Pray for an increase of love for others.

CHARACTERISTICS OF A CHRISTOPHER (B)

Pray for others. This means of being a Christopher is at the disposal of *all*. There are no exceptions. Not only can we pray for ourselves, for others whom we know—we can pray for the great majority in our country and over the world who have little or no knowledge of Christ. Even one minute a day of prayer would count for much.

One woman we know spends an hour each day in St. Patrick's Cathedral praying for the Secretary of State that he may in his official duties uphold the Christian principles upon which this country was founded. All of us can follow her example, using this most powerful means to change the world for the better.

". . . *and pray for one another, that you may be saved. For the continual prayer of a just man availeth much.*" (James 5:16)

⋙ Lord, teach me to devote more time to prayer for others.

CHARACTERISTICS OF A CHRISTOPHER (C)

By going to all men. One of the greatest tributes to Christ was that *"He went about doing good."* Following His example, we, too, must mingle with "all men" who know Him not, whether they live in the crowded cities or in the sparsely settled rural areas. It is absolutely necessary for us to go to *them*—to bring Christ to them. They will not come to us. They have just as much right to His blessings as we have. They are entitled to them. If they reject them, that is their responsibility. We have a serious obligation at least to offer them.

"There must be something wrong," said one person, *"with those who can be so perfect in the practice of what they hold to be the true religion and yet show so little interest in sharing it with others."* This should be a challenge to every Christopher.

"For thou shalt be his witness to all men, of all things which thou hast seen and heard." (Acts 22:15)

❧ Lord, help me to imitate Thee in going about doing good.

CHARACTERISTICS OF A CHRISTOPHER (D)

By transmitting principles. A Christopher always will give a good example, but far more than that is needed. Christ meant that we should pass on His fundamental principles when He told the disciples to *"preach the gospel to every creature."*

Ideas change the world. The wrong ideas of the totalitarian state, spread far and wide, even in our own country, have infected the lives of hundreds of millions. Until people like *you* bring the right ideas to these misguided people, the infection will remain. If we had the cure for cancer and people were dying of it, how long would we hesitate to bring it to them? Positive action must be taken, and the sooner the better.

"And when it was day, going out he went into a desert place, and the multitudes sought him, and came unto him: and they stayed him that he should not depart from them. To whom he said: To other cities also I must preach the kingdom of God: for therefore am I sent." (Luke 4:42–43)

✠ Pray that increasingly you may go to others to bring them the fundamental teachings of Christ.

NEVER ENOUGH

The mystery of a ten-year series of mail thefts from charitable organizations was solved recently with the arrest of a quiet, unassuming mail clerk, who had served for forty-two years in the New York Post Office. Though he could have retired with two-thirds salary six years ago, the man stayed on working in order to continue his stealing. He wanted, he said, *"to build up a little nest egg."*

The story is common enough, unfortunately. There are many people who are dissatisfied, whether they have a little or a lot. Yet just as there is no wrongdoing that does not hurt others, so there is no wrongdoing that can ever give us true security or contentment. Real happiness can be achieved only when we make the most of the situation we are in, and then follow through by doing the most we can for those less fortunate.

"The thief cometh not, but for to steal, and to kill, and to destroy. I am come that they may have life, and may have it more abundantly." (John 10:10)

⟞ Pray that your vision may be broadened so that you will see the tremendous harm you might do by a single, selfish act.

"MINIMUM EFFORT, MAXIMUM PLEASURE"

Some years ago the late Dr. Alexis Carrel made an interesting statement about the need for self-discipline. *"Everything has been made too easy for most of us,"* he said. *"All life has aspired to the condition of . . . minimum effort and maximum pleasure. Amusement has been the national cry; 'a good time' our chief concern. The perfect life as viewed by the average youth or adult is a round of ease or entertainment . . . This indolent and undisciplined way of life has sapped our individual vigor, imperiled our democratic form of government . . . Our race pitifully needs new supplies of discipline, morality, and intelligence."*

Of course a *reasonable* share of pleasure is intended for each of us: God wants us to have it. But we must keep in mind that we are here only for a short time to prepare for eternity. Once secure in that knowledge, temperance will come much easier.

"And when the last hour comes, you will begin to think very differently of your whole past life; and be exceedingly sorry that you have been so negligent and reckless." (Imitation of Christ I:23, 20)

⊸§ Lord, let me seek out the difficult things of this life that I may take my eternal ease in the life to come.

NOT THROUGH YET

A man on a hiking trip through the Blue Ridge Mountains came to the top of a hill and saw, just below the crest, a small log cabin. Its aged owner was sitting in front of the door, smoking a corncob pipe, and when the traveler drew close enough he asked the old man patronizingly: *"Lived here all your life?"*

"Nope," the old mountaineer replied patiently. *"Not yet."*

However long or short it may be, there is time ahead for all of us to live our days with high purpose. When we lose this sense of purpose in life, we have lost an important part of life itself. Living each day fully is a vital part of being a Christopher.

"Be not therefore solicitous for tomorrow; for the morrow will be solicitous for itself." (Matthew 6:34)

Pray that you may be ever aware that each day is a lifetime to be lived for Christ.

TREMENDOUS TRIFLES

A friend of ours was recently advised to take better care of his teeth if he wished to avoid serious trouble in the future. For several weeks he followed the dentist's instructions regularly. Then, as so often happens, he began to grow careless. Soon, as far as practical application was concerned, the dentist's advice seemed to be forgotten altogether. At the next annual checkup, X rays revealed the natural consequences of our friend's neglect. His teeth were in worse shape than ever before.

"You've no one but yourself to blame," the dentist informed him. *"Proper tooth care can add ten years to anyone's life . . . and improper care can shorten it to the same extent."*

The little things in life seem so uninteresting. Yet trifles can be tremendous in their consequences. Success results from a multiplication of little things.

"Well done, good and faithful servant! Thou hast been faithful over a little, I will set thee over much. Enter into the joy of thy lord." (Matthew 25:23)

⊷ Pray that you may be ever faithful in small things so that the "big things"—your eternal salvation—may not be denied you.

THE PRICE OF LIBERTY

Almost everyone admires the virtue of self-control, whether he practices it or not. The disciplined man is a joy to himself and to most others. He has that strength we value most highly—that which comes from inner mastery.

To remain calm when the temptation to show temper is strong; to be honest when it would be easy to do something a little underhanded; to be kind when it would be easy to hurt someone—these are the marks of character.

Oddly enough, the man who restrains himself is free, while the unrestrained man is a slave to his own confusion. As Daniel Webster put it: *"Liberty exists in proportion to wholesome restraint."*

In short, a person who controls himself merits the blessings of God and man, not to speak of the pleasure he gives himself.

"Blessed is he that could have transgressed and hath not transgressed, and could do evil things, and hath not done them." (Ecclesiasticus 31:10)

&§ O Lord, grant that millions now drifting in the shallows of self-indulgence may launch out into the rough seas of self-discipline.

"THE LAST THREAD"

In a New York court a desperate father whose son was being tried as a juvenile delinquent openly confessed that despite all that had been done for the boy—and he and his wife thought they had done almost everything possible—it had all been in vain. *"Your Honor,"* the father said finally, *"we'll have to give the boy up—disown him. I don't see what else we can do."*

"If you desert your son now," the judge told him, *"you'll lose him forever. You'll break the last thread of hope—his faith in you. Without that faith, he'll be hopeless."*

Rejection of those who offend us solves nothing. It doesn't help the offender; and it doesn't help us, either, since we invariably suffer. If Christ does not disown sinners, surely we can follow His example.

"And if anyone have caused grief . . . you should rather forgive him and comfort him, lest perhaps such a one be swallowed up with overmuch sorrow." (II Corinthians 2:5–7)

⊷§ Help me to recall, O Lord, that before I reject anyone as "lost" I should remember that I have not done everything I can to save him.

WHO IS MY NEIGHBOR?

G. K. Chesterton was not merely joking when he wrote, *"The Bible tells us to love our neighbors, and also to love our enemies; probably because they are generally the same people."*

Sometimes when we hear that modern communications and transportation have brought people closer together, we forget that the worst wars in history have occurred in just this period of heightened contact.

The mere act of bringing people closer together in physical and intellectual contact will never of itself guarantee harmony. There must be, first of all, spiritual contact, a sharing in the same realization that we have all been created by the same Father and for the same purpose.

"But I say to you, Love your enemies: do good to them that hate you: and pray for them that persecute and calumniate you: That you may be the children of your Father who is in heaven, who maketh his sun to rise upon the good, and bad, and raineth upon the just and the unjust." (Matthew 5:44–45)

&⚬ Lord, help us to love all our enemies, especially the "foes of our own household."

BE YOURSELF!

A photographer who aimed to please everybody once advertised: *"As you look to me, $1.00; as you think you look, $1.50; as you would like to look, $2.00."*

Most of us get into one sort of trouble or another because we try to fool ourselves. There is the everlasting temptation to pretend to be something we are not. Many headaches can be avoided by following the simple advice: *"Be yourself!"* If God gives us only one talent, He wants us to use it efficiently; but He certainly does not wish us to try to fool the public, to give the impression that we have five or ten talents. Of a young businessman who had unusual success, despite certain limitations, someone wisely said, *"He is smart enough to know what he doesn't know."*

Conceit can trip any of us. It can even destroy us if we exaggerate self, forgetting that anything and everything we have, little or much, comes from God.

⊷§ Pray for the grace never to deceive yourself.

KEEP JUMPING

"May I ask you the secret of success?" an ambitious young man said to a successful merchant.

"There is no easy or simple secret," the merchant answered. *"You must be on the alert for little things and jump at opportunities."*

"But how can I tell the opportunities when they come?"

"You can't," the merchant said tartly. *"You just have to keep jumping."*

Every day presents us with countless opportunities for success in this life and in eternity. More often than not we let them pass, judging them too small to be important. But no situation is unimportant or small if we see it clearly, make proper use of it. If we are spiritually alert, life is a constant progress toward our eternal goal.

"Look to yourselves, that you lose not the things which you have wrought: but that you may receive a full reward." (II John 1:8)

⊷ Pray that you may be constantly alive to each opportunity to do God's Will.

HE STUCK WITH IT!

A recent story tells of a man who has almost reached the zenith of worldly contentment. He is a farmer who made his fortune in that most unlikely of all places, the Dust Bowl. Flat broke in 1933 and his farm a wind-blown desert, with uncommon courage he *"stayed with his land."* When slight success had been achieved, he launched out, got into new enterprises on and off the farm. He not only turned a desolation into a paradise but soon found himself worth $500,000!

This sort of confidence, the willingness to make the first simple effort, and the ability to "follow through," often spells the difference between failure and success for eternity.

All we have to do to get the power we need is to connect a line to the Spiritual Powerhouse—God. What many lack is the faith that *"it can be done."* It is the secret of success—material or spiritual—first of all to have faith and then to put it to work.

"I can do all things in Him who strengtheneth me." (Philippians 4:13)

◦§ Give me the will to do what Thou willest, then command what Thou wilt.

GET MOVING

Full of meaning for every Christopher are the words of the gospel describing the ascension of Christ:

"At length, He was manifested to the eleven themselves as they were taking a meal. . . .
"And He said to them. 'Go out into the whole world, and proclaim the Gospel to all creation. He who believes and is baptized shall be saved, but he who believes not shall be condemned. . . .
"So, then, the Lord Jesus, after He had discoursed with them, was taken up into Heaven, and sat at God's right hand. But they went forth and preached everywhere, the Lord working with them. . . ." (Mark 16: 14-15; 19-20)

The Acts of the Apostles continues the story:

". . . and you shall be My witnesses both in Jerusalem and in all Judea and Samaria, and to the remotest part of the earth.
"And having said this, while they were looking on He was taken up, and a cloud received Him out of their sight. And while they were gazing intently into heaven as He went, behold, two men in white robes were standing beside them, who moreover said, 'Men of Galilee, why do you stand gazing up into heaven? . . ." (Acts 1: 8-11)

To the last Our Lord urged His followers to *"Go out into the whole world . . ."* No sooner had He disappeared than His angels appeared and reminded them to stop "gazing" and get started on their big world job.

⊷§ Lord, let me never fail to bring Thy love to all within my reach.

EACH TO HIS OWN

A bricklayer whose brother happened to be a gifted and famous violinist once found himself in conversation with the head of the construction company for which he worked.

"It must be fine to have such a renowned man for a brother," the executive observed. And then, anxious not to offend his worker's pride, he continued: *"Of course we must accept the fact that talent isn't evenly distributed— even in the same family."*

"That's the truth," came back the reply. *"Why, my brother doesn't know the first thing about bricklaying. It's a good thing he can afford to pay others to build his house for him."*

It's not vanity to recognize our own place in life and our fitness for it. Instead of wasting our time envying others their talents, we should devote ourselves to the productive use of our own ability. God intends each of us for a special job, and He gives us the right tools.

"Then he also who had received the two talents came and said, 'My lord, thou didst intrust me with two talents; see I have made two talents more!' His master said to him, 'Well done, good and faithful servant! Thou hast been faithful over a little, I will set thee over much. Enter in the joy of thy Lord!'" (Matthew 25: 22, 23)

⊷§ Lord, help me to recognize the talents Thou hast given me, and to put them to work for Thee.

FACE THE FACTS

A young boy who had shot and killed four children was asked why he did it. *"I always wondered what it would be like to kill somebody,"* came the reply.

The examining board to which he was sent before trial decided he was *"possessed of a mental condition which could affect his criminal responsibility."* But one of the board members, in a dissenting opinion, stated that the boy was still *personally responsible* for his crime.

There is today an increasingly dangerous tendency to evade the facts—to place all the blame for all sin on anything and everything *except one's own personal choice,* one's own free, responsible act of will.

When a person continually offers evasive excuses for his own misdeeds, he eventually becomes entangled in his own rationalizations. It is much more practical to be honest about the situation and face the facts. And to do this will help eliminate additional trouble in the future.

"If we say that we have no sin, we deceive ourselves, and the truth is not in us." (I John 1:8)

&c§ Lord, give me an honest willingness to take the consequences of my deliberate decisions.

DOORS OF DESTINY

A member of the Department of Housing and Buildings was explaining the tragic Cocoanut Grove disaster of 1943. *"There was nothing wrong with the planning of that club,"* he said. *"It had the proper number of exits. The trouble was that except for the revolving door in front, all the exits were locked and the revolving door jammed. If the exits had been open, a few people might have died in the first flare-up, but not four hundred and ninety-two."*

Our own lives are so busy and so crowded with minor preoccupations that we frequently overlook the big things. And through our neglect of the things that really matter, we might be locking and jamming the only doors through which we can be rescued for eternity. This is something which merits our frequent reflection and prayer.

"How shall we escape if we neglect so great salvation?" (Hebrews 2:3)

♋ Pray that you will see the importance of the door into eternity and will not obstruct the entrance with the debris of sin.

"I CRIED MYSELF TO SLEEP"

In one of the battles of the Civil War when his army was suffering a severe defeat, General Lee rode over a section of the battlefield where the fighting had passed on. As he did so, a wounded Northern soldier in the spirit of defiance lifted his head and shouted: *"Hurrah for the Union."*

The soldier then expected to be shot, but instead Lee dismounted and said simply, *"I'm sorry that you are so gravely wounded. I hope you may soon be well."*

Afterward the soldier said: *"That spirit broke my heart, and I cried myself to sleep."*

Often others are hateful to us only because they expect unkindness and are anticipating it. When they receive instead a word or a gesture of friendship, they are defenceless and quickly ready to return the kindness they are given. Just as hatred breeds hatred, so love creates love.

"Love your enemies, do good to them that hate you." (Luke 6:27)

⊸§ Give me, Lord, an understanding sympathy even for those who mistakenly hate the truth.

A KING INDEED

Frederick the Great of Prussia was walking along a road on the outskirts of Berlin one day when accidentally he brushed against a very old man. *"Who are you?"* Frederick asked out of idle curiosity as the two came to a halt.

"I am a king," the old man answered.

"A king?" echoed Frederick. *"Over what principality do you reign?"*

"Over myself," was the proud reply. *"I rule myself because I control myself. I am my own subject to command."*

All of us can be kings, in the sense of the old man's words. But how many of us actually are? Instead of being in command, often we let ourselves be ruled over by the tyrants of temper or laziness or passion. We cannot hope to influence others if we are, as the common expression puts it, "not ourselves." And we can only be ourselves by controlling ourselves.

"A horse not broken becometh stubborn, and a child left to himself will become headstrong." (Ecclesiasticus 30:8)

Lord, help me to rule over my passions, that Thou mayest rule over me.

YOU NEED THESE THREE

In his absorbing pamphlet, *Apostles All,* Father Richard Rooney, S.J., lists three "faiths" which anyone who would play the role of a Christ-bearer *should possess.*

a. *Faith in Your Cause.* A man can hardly win others to a cause in which he himself believes only half-heartedly. Unless *he* personally is completely "sold" on it, his words will lack conviction and sincerity. . . . He will not have the enthusiasm needed to set others on fire.

b. *Faith in Oneself.* Nothing hinders the winning of others more than a lack of faith in yourself. Men search both your face and soul to see if what you are trying to draw them to has given *you* the qualities they want: dependability, self-reliance, courage. If they find these in you, they will listen to you further. . . .

c. *Faith in Others.* One of the most painful experiences of youth is the heartbreak that comes when they find that their elders, especially their parents, do not trust them, have no faith in them. That lost feeling never completely dies, even in adulthood. Old and young need trust. No man can lead others, even to Christ, unless he shows them that he believes in them.

❧ Help us, Lord, to increase our faith in You, in Your cause, in ourselves, and in others, that we may be better prepared to bring You to all men.

THE GREATEST OF ALL

A radio commentator some time ago devoted most of his fifteen-minute network program to St. Paul's celebrated eulogy on the necessity of love above all things. It might prove to your advantage to ponder it frequently and prayerfully.

"If I spoke the languages of men and of angels, but had not love, I should sound as a blaring trumpet, or a clashing cymbal.

"And if I possessed prophetic powers, and knew all mysteries and all science, and if I possessed entire faith, so as to remove mountains, but had not love I should be nothing.

"And if I gave bit by bit all my possessions to feed the poor, and if I delivered up my body to be burned, but had not love, it would avail me nothing.

"Love is long-suffering, is kind; love envies not, boasts not of itself, is not arrogant, is not rude, is not self-seeking, is not provoked to anger, takes no account of evil treatment, rejoices not over wickedness, but rejoices with the truth. Love bears everything, believes everything, hopes everything, endures everything." (I Corinthians 13: 1–7) (continued tomorrow)

�§ Pour forth upon us, O Lord, the spirit of Thy charity.

THE GREATEST OF ALL (*continued*)

"*Love never fails; but whether there be prophetic powers, they shall come to an end; or languages, they shall cease; or knowledge, it shall be rendered useless. For we know but partially, and we prophesy but partially; but when the perfect arrives, then the partial shall come to an end.*

"*When I was a child I spoke as a child, I felt as a child, I thought as a child; now that I have become a man I have discarded childish ways.*

"*For now we see in a mirror, dimly; but then face to face. Now I know partially; but then I shall know completely, even as I am completely known.*

And now there remain faith, hope, love—these three; but the greatest of these is love." (I Corinthians 13: 8–13)

⋰§ O God, enlighten our hearts and refresh them abundantly with the sweetness of perfect charity.

CREDIT WHERE IT'S DUE

During a rehearsal of Beethoven's Ninth Symphony the members of the orchestra were so overwhelmingly moved by the conducting of Arturo Toscanini that they rose as one man and applauded him. When the spontaneous cheering had subsided Toscanini turned to his men, tears glistening in his eyes.

"Please . . . please! Don't do this!" he said in a pathetic voice. *"You see, gentlemen, it isn't me you should applaud. It's Beethoven!"*

Every Christopher would do well to cultivate a profound respect for the achievements of others while still retaining a modest awareness of one's own accomplishments.

In bearing Christ to those who do not know Him, we can be modest, show them respect, and still never compromise with the Truth. After all, Christ meant their eternal destiny to be the same as ours!

"But the wisdom, that is from above, first indeed is chaste, then peaceable, modest, easy to be persuaded, consenting to the good, full of mercy and good fruits, without judging, without dissimulation." (James 3:17)

꿐 Blessed be God; blessed be His Holy Name; blessed be Jesus Christ, true God and true Man.

YOU PAY THE PRICE

Medical scientists are daily learning more about the mysterious influence for good or ill that our minds exert over our bodies. Chronic indigestion, for instance—a source of real misery—is often caused by some emotional or mental tangle, say an increasing number of modern specialists.

And as they delve deeper into the relationship between body and mind, some state further that a healthy spiritual outlook on life—cheerfulness, courage, kindness, love of one's neighbors—is absolutely essential to our well-being. These authorities are daily discovering the harmful physical effects of envy, doubt, fear, hatred, jealousy, and greed. They know that wrong attitudes and false desires can make one physically sick.

Our chief job is to "seek first the kingdom of God and His justice." We are not thereby automatically assured of health of mind and body, but it is certainly true that those who live for God achieve a tranquillity of spirit in this life as well as happiness hereafter. It should give many even greater incentive to practice virtue when they realize that not only their earthly well-being but also their eternal welfare is at stake.

"A joyful mind maketh age flourishing: a sorrowful spirit drieth up the bones." (Proverbs 17:22)

❧ Pray for those who are suffering in body and soul.

GOOD SENSE

In Hollywood not so long ago a program director of the National Broadcasting Company volunteered his impressions of the Christophers when he heard what several acquaintances who had become imbued with the idea were doing. *"You know,"* he told one of them, *"this Christopher thing has terrific possibilities. I'm not a Catholic myself, but what you're driving at makes good sense. There's a bit of the missionary in every one of us. The trouble is that so far about the only ones working hard at it have been the fellows upsetting the world."*

Summed up in those few sentences is the conviction of every sincere bearer of Christ. The command of Our Lord: "go ye into the whole world" can be fulfilled more quickly and completely if all play a part to this end to the best of their abilities. The Christophers' simple formula aims, therefore, at getting *little* people to do *big* things—encouraging the average person to reach beyond his or her own small circle for the big world outside. Only when large numbers do this can mankind the earth over be won back to Christ.

"For the sons of the world are more clever in their own sphere than are the sons of the light." (Luke 16:8)

⮦ Lord, teach me not to spare myself in carrying your love and truth to the world as far as I can reach.

TURN ABOUT

Sometimes it is hard to understand why those who flout the rules of the game of life seem to prosper. Yet when the going is particularly hard, it often helps to read a reminder like the following, written by Gerard Groote about 1384:

"Then will the poor and humble have great confidence; while the proud will be taken with great fear on every side.

"Then will it be seen that he was wise in this world, who had learned to be a fool and to be despised for God's sake.

"Then will every affliction patiently undergone delight us.

"Then will every devout man rejoice; and the ungodly will mourn.

"Then will the mortified flesh rejoice more than if it had always bathed in delights.

"Then will the despised garment shine brightly; and the costly robe be vile.

"Then will constant patience avail more than all worldly power.

"Then will simple obedience be exalted above all worldly cunning.

"Then will a pure conscience cause greater joy than learned philosophy.

"Then will the contempt of riches have more weight, and will profit more, than all the treasures of the earth."
—(*Imitation of Christ* 1: 24, 20)

&§ O Lord, keep me reminded that I must not to try to have my heaven on earth.

CAMPAIGN OF HATE

Those who strive to wreck the world and are working night and day to prepare our destruction aim first of all to destroy all knowledge and love of God. That they do not confine their efforts to the destruction of any particular religion but rather religion as such is shown in the statement of V. Stepanov, a translator of Marx:

"We need a resolute struggle against the priest, whether he be called the pastor, the abbot, the rabbi, the patriarch, the mullah, or the Pope. At a certain stage this struggle must be transformed into the struggle against God, whether He be called Jehovah, Jesus, Buddha, or Allah."

This war against God is a war against the children of God also. It is the image of God in each human being which those who hate religion wish to destroy. And since such a hatred exists, that should be reason enough to make all of us willing to answer their malevolent zeal with our intense love and to surpass their efforts for evil with our work for good.

"The fool hath said in his heart: There is no God. They are corrupt, and are become abominable in their ways: there is none that doth good, no not one." (Psalm 13:1)

⊷ Lord, help me to work harder *for* Thee, than those who hate Thee work *against* Thee.

FAR FROM WASTED

A reporter called on Thomas A. Edison one afternoon to interview him about a substitute for lead in the manufacture of storage batteries that the scientist was seeking. Edison informed the man he had made 20,000 experiments but none of them had worked.

"But aren't you discouraged by all this waste of effort?" the reporter asked, amazed. *"Waste!"* exclaimed Mr. Edison, *"There's nothing wasted. I have discovered 20,000 things that won't work."*

From time to time we may feel that some good action of ours has not borne fruit. But we should not be discouraged: easy success is more likely to harm us than gradual achievement. And often an action that may seem in vain can have a delayed, important effect, like a seed ripening into grain.

Every spiritual act directed toward God is guaranteed its effect as far as our own spiritual welfare is concerned.

"But he that received the seed upon good ground, is he that heareth the word, and understandeth, and beareth fruit, and yieldeth the one an hundredfold, and another sixty, and another thirty." (Matthew 13:23)

ᴥᶳ Pray for the foresight and patience to persevere.

SINS OF OMISSION

"And in the morning, returning into the city he was hungry. And seeing a certain fig tree by the wayside, he came to it, and found nothing on it but leaves only, and he saith to it: May no fruit grow on thee henceforward forever. And immediately the fig tree withered away."
(Matthew 21:18–19)

At first glance this parable might seem unnecessarily cruel, since the fig tree was doing no harm. Still, it wasn't doing good. Therefore the symbolic nature of Christ's act becomes clear and deeply meaningful. The tree had plenty of beautiful foliage, yet the purpose for which it was created—to bear fruit—was not being fulfilled. So Christ decreed that it should wither and die.

Many go through life like the fig tree: apparently doing no harm, but not doing any good either. They bury their talents and bear no fruit.

For those about to graduate and commence their life's work there is much food for thought in those words of Our Lord. After reflecting, they should pray not merely to *be* good, but also to *do* good.

◈ Lord, keep me from committing sins of omission.

LOOK UP, NOT DOWN

Back in the days of sailing ships an inexperienced seaman was sent aloft in a storm to disentangle a length of broken rigging from the mainmast. His body lashed by the raging wind, the youngster climbed up swiftly and did the job. As he started down again, he happened to look below him at the angry sea and the rolling deck.

"I'm falling," he shouted, as his grip weakened.

"Don't look down, boy! Look up!" the mate called from the deck below.

The boy forced himself to turn his head and look above him. Calm and reassured, he made his way back to the deck.

If in a panic we decide that we cannot maintain the high level we have achieved, all we need do is look up to God with trust and humility. His arm will steady us.

"O Lord my God in thee have I put my trust . . ."
(Psalm 7:2)

⇜§ Pray for childlike confidence in God.

154

NOT LICKED YET

A gentleman walking along the street passed a vacant lot where some boys were playing baseball. He asked one of the youngsters what the score was.

"We're behind, eighteen to nothing," was the answer.

"Well," said the gentleman, "I must say you don't look very discouraged."

"Discouraged?" the boy said, puzzled, "We're not discouraged. We haven't come to bat yet!"

There is a thought in this little anecdote that could cheer us all: on those days when life seems to be defeating us, when small trials come in a series, we can then think of life as a kind of baseball game, and patiently wait our turn at bat. Moreover, we can have the confidence of a winning team, since we have a Captain incapable of failure.

"But in all these things we overcome, because of Him that hath loved us." (Romans 8:37)

෴Pray that God will give you the confidence which comes from implicit trust in Him.

AS A MAN THINKETH

A young lady went into a bookstore and asked the clerk: *"Have you Irving Stone's book,* Immoral Wife?"

"The title is Immortal Wife," the clerk replied. *"I'll get it for you."*

"Oh, please don't bother," came back the startling answer. *"If that's the correct name of the book, I don't believe I'd care for it! I had something else in mind."*

Such an attitude as this reader's is typical of the trend toward intellectual immorality which is debasing the minds of many. Wittingly or not, people in increasing numbers are allowing themselves to be *"mentally seduced"* into accepting the pagan philosophy that the Nazis taught and which the Communists still follow. The goal of Christ's enemies is so to defile our minds that we will lose all respect for our bodies. And when that happens, Christian morality ceases to have any meaning. *"As a man thinketh, so is he,"* runs the old saying. It is part of the tactics of the godless to put this thought to their own use for their own evil purposes.

"But I say to you, that whosoever shall look on a woman to lust after her, hath already committed adultery with her in his heart." (Matthew 5:28)

꙾ Keep me clean of heart, O Lord, that I may see Thy divine beauty in every human being.

A HIGH PRICE

In these days the value of chastity is more and more being questioned. Enemies of normal decency advance many arguments. But they all fall flat when considered in the light of the Word of God. St. Paul put it down very plainly that those who defy God on this important point pay a severe penalty in the long run:

1. *"For they that are according to the flesh, mind the things that are of the flesh, but they that are according to the spirit, mind the things that are of the spirit.*

"For the wisdom of the flesh is death; but the wisdom of the spirit is life and peace.

"Because the wisdom of the flesh is an enemy to God, for it is not subject to the law of God, neither can it be.

"And they who are in the flesh, cannot please God. . . . For if you live according to the flesh, you shall die; but if by the Spirit, you mortify the deeds of the flesh, you shall live." (Roman 8:5–8, 13)

2. *"Know you not that you are the temple of God, and that the Spirit of God dwelleth in you? But if any man violate the temple of God, him shall God destroy."* (I Corinthians 3:16–17)   (continued tomorrow)

⇜ Pray for the grace always to be "clean of heart."

A HIGH PRICE (*continued*)

In the Old Testament there are constant reminders that no one wins in the game of misusing the body. Here is one of the most telling:

"*Mind not the deceit of a woman.*

"*For the lips of a harlot are like a honeycomb dropping, and her throat is smoother than oil.*

"*But her end is bitter as wormwood, and sharp as a two-edged sword.*

"*Her feet go down into death, and her steps go in as far as hell.*

"*They walk not by the path of life, her steps are wandering, and unaccountable.*

"*Now, therefore, my son, hear me, and depart not from the words of my mouth.*

"*Remove thy way far from her, and come not nigh the doors of her house.*

"*Give not thy honor to strangers, and thy years to the cruel.*

"*Lest strangers be filled with thy strength, and thy labors be in another man's house.*

"*And thou mourn at the last, when thou shalt have spent thy flesh and thy body, and say:*

"'*Why have I hated instruction, and my heart consented not to reproof.*'

"'*And have not heard the voice of them that taught me, and have not inclined my ear to masters?*'" (Proverbs 5:2-13)

❧ O Jesus, teach me to use my body according to Thy law and never to abuse it.

FALSE SECURITY

On the left-hand side of a newspaper page some time back was a close-up of one of the most horrible hotel fires of recent history. Above the picture of men, women, and children cowering on smoke-surrounded ledges, shrinking from the flames, was this searing caption: *"People Aren't Fireproof!"*

Reason for the strong wording was contained in the account of the blaze, and the facts presented were terrifying. There was violation after violation of fire ordinances, carelessness, and stupidity. *"The sixty-one people who died in the ——— Hotel perhaps thought they were safe. Its twenty-one-storied layers of steel and reinforced concrete were fire resistant—but architects and decorators had built a potential funeral pyre inside."*

It's easy to feel secure, to be certain of ourselves, to think we are safe. Yet, as architects of our own destiny, many of us have built the *external* structure of our spiritual lives without paying enough attention to the interior. What a sad awakening is in store for those who wait to die before doing anything.

"Wherefore he that thinketh himself to stand, let him take heed lest he fall." (I Corinthians 10: 12)

🙠 Lord, let me place all my trust in Thee, and from Thee get my strength.

ONE SMALL LIGHT

Some time ago I had occasion to visit the Metropolitan Opera House in New York. It was late at night, after the performance, and all the employees except the assistant manager had gone home. He asked me to wait until he could turn on the main lights and went down the aisle and mounted the stage alone.

As I waited, scarcely able to see the outline of his figure in the darkness, there was the sound of a match striking wood, then a tiny sliver of light appeared. Yet small as it was, it was greater than all the blackness around it. After that it was but the work of a moment to multiply its minute glow thousands of times and dispel the shadows which still remained. With the click of a switch, clusters of electric lights flooded the Opera House, and the darkness was gone.

The least person, no matter how insignificant he may feel, who is interested in bringing the light of Christ's truth to the whole world, is a pinpoint of light in the darkness, greater than all the encircling gloom. Darkness disappears in the same proportion as light is added. It is as simple as that.

"You are the light of the world . . ." (Matthew 5:14)

❧ Lord, strengthen me to do my part in bearing Thy light to all mankind.

WHERE ARE YOU GOING?

An American riding on a train in northern China found the behavior of a native vendor extremely interesting. There was nothing unusual about the man's appearance, but he seemed to be having an odd effect on the other passengers. He leaned over each of them in turn, extolling his wares, but didn't make one sale. Despite that, he would ask each person some further question, and the answer invariably was a startled look on the passenger's face.

Finally the American's curiosity led him to call the vendor over and ask him what it was that upset the travelers.

"Well," the native explained, "I ask them: 'Where are you going?' and they usually answer, naming this city or that.

"But then I tell them that isn't what I meant—that what I meant was: 'Where are you going when you die?'

"It seems to make everyone of them stop and think!"

This is, admittedly, an odd way of being an apostle, a Christopher, and helping others for eternity—but it still is a way!

"Watch ye therefore, because you know not the day nor the hour." (Matthew 25:13)

◆§ Pray that you may become more and more aware of the eternity of reward or punishment which awaits you, and that you may pass this awareness on to others.

LITTLE TO SHOW

A young woman who has entertained in most of the leading supper clubs told us not long ago that she found a striking similarity in all the conversations of successful businessmen when they have been drinking just enough to make them talkative.

Inevitably, she says, they come to the point where they start to bemoan that *they have little to show for their lives.* They insist that their wealth and position do not count for much. Instead, they confide that life is empty for them because they feel they have done little to make the world better than they found it.

They recognize that they have somehow missed out in what matters most—achievement not for self alone, but for love of God and of fellow men. Had these men grasped their early opportunities to do good, they might now know peace. They would realize the meaning of the words of the gospel:

"You have not chosen me: but I have chosen you; and have appointed you, that you should go, and should bring forth fruit; and your fruit should remain; that whatsoever you shall ask of the Father in my name, he may give it you." (John 15:16)

⊷ Pray that millions who are leading empty lives will learn to make them full by filling the lives of others.

WHY HITLER FAILED

In his book, *I Paid Hitler*, Fritz Thyssen, the German industrialist, points out the chief reason for Hitler's failure to conquer Europe:

"Hitler had an unprecedented opportunity, such as no man will ever again be offered so easily, to create something entirely new. However, besides the fact that he knows absolutely nothing about matters economic, he cannot even fully understand his economic advisers . . . His constant worry has ever been to keep himself in power . . . he believes that he alone is a great man, and all others non-entities."

This self-absorption of Hitler accounted in large measure for his defeat. Since he did not believe in the dignity of man, created in the image of God, he believed only in himself. And, like all those who believe only in themselves, Hitler shut himself off from the enrichment of spirit and intellect that comes when we are willing to receive what others have to give.

❧ Lord, keep me always aware of the dignity of man, created in Thy image.

SOLID FOUNDATIONS

Some months ago work was begun on a new building on Park Avenue in New York City. At first things proceeded very slowly. Excavation for the foundation seemed endless. Day after day, week after week, the huge steam shovels dug deep into the ground, biting huge pieces of earth with their steel jaws, until one began to wonder if there ever would be a building erected at all . . . if there ever would be anything more than an immense hole in the ground.

But at last the work was completed and on the site there began to rise one of the newest and most modern skyscrapers in America—truly a "miracle of production."

So it is with the framework of our own lives. Just as no building can rise in strength and grandeur without a sound, solid foundation, neither can we hope for eternal success unless we sink our spiritual foundations deep and thus make strong and rich our hope for happiness in the life to come.

"Everyone therefore that heareth these My words, and doth them, shall be likened to a wise man that built his house upon a rock." (Matthew 7:24)

§ Give me to know the depth of my own nothingness, that I may rise to the heights of Thy love.

ALL SUMMED UP

Love of God is not just some vague expression of sentiment. Neither does it mean that God should be loved on a half-hearted basis. He should be loved with the *whole* of one's being. And on this point the words of Christ Himself are most explicit:

> *"Thou shalt love the Lord thy God*
> *with thy whole heart,*
> *and with thy whole soul,*
> *and with thy whole mind.*
> *This is the greatest and the first commandment."*

Then, as regards our relationship with our fellow man, Christ added:

> *"And the second is like to this:*
> *Thou shalt love thy neighbor as thyself.*
> *On these two commandments dependeth the*
> *whole law and the prophets."*
> (Matthew 22: 37–40)

If anyone say, therefore, that he loves God yet hates his neighbor, he is deceiving himself. But, more than that, he is laying himself open to eternal punishment for violating the Law of God as set forth in His Commandments.

Dear God, take my heart in love of Thee; and give me Thy heart to love my neighbor.

FAIR EXCHANGE

At a crowded intersection while waiting for the light to change, a car stalled, holding up a line of other vehicles behind it. Obviously flustered, the man who was driving the car hurriedly got out and lifted the hood of the engine to investigate; and, as he did, the driver of the car behind began honking his horn.

The noise kept on without letup until the driver of the stalled car, still meeting with no success in his attempts to discover the trouble, suddenly straightened up and spoke to the impatient motorist behind him.

"If you'll fix my car," he said calmly, *"I'll be glad to keep blowing your horn for you."*

In our own impatience we sometimes think that mere noises will make a bad situation right itself. We think that if we shout loud enough everyone will be bound to hear and lend a hand.

Actually, impatience over trivial annoyances often makes matters worse. On the other hand, realistic appraisal of the situation and considered, thoughtful action are the best guarantee of quick, profitable results.

"A mild answer breaketh wrath: but a harsh word stirreth up fury." (Proverbs 15:1)

⋧ O Lord, teach me to be as calm and patient with others as Thou art with me.

YOU GET AS YOU GIVE

High up in the Rockies there lived a small boy and his mother. One day, after he had been punished severely, the lad ran to the edge of a precipice and shouted back at his mother, *"I hate you! I hate you!"* Across the ravine came the echo: *"I hate you! I hate you!"*

Thoroughly frightened, the boy ran back to his mother, and sobbed: *"Who is that bad man over there who shouted, 'I hate you'?"*

Taking the boy's hand, the mother led him back to the edge of the precipice. *"Now, sonny,"* she said, *"call out, 'I love you! I love you!'"* The little boy did as he was told. Clearly and sweetly the echo came, repeating his words.

"My child," said the mother, taking the child into her arms, *"that is the law of life—what you give, you get."*

"Cast thy bread upon the running waters: for after a long time thou shalt find it again." (Ecclesiastes 11:1)

&⸹ O Lord, teach me to be as interested in "giving" as I am in "getting."

GOOD TO DO

One of the characters in Shakespeare's *The Merchant of Venice* gives us a sound piece of advice about practicing what we preach:

"If to do were as easy as to know what were good to do, chapels had been churches and poor men's cottages princes' palaces. It is a good divine that follows his own instructions: I can easier teach twenty what were good to be done, than be one of the twenty to follow mine own teaching."

In short: actions speak louder than words. If we want others to do good, we should do it ourselves first. Not only is that the best way to teach, but at the same time it is the best way for us to learn.

An act of kindness, a sympathetic word or act, is the best teacher. In the same play Shakespeare states this truth forcefully:

"How far that little candle throws its beams: So shines a good deed in a naughty world."

◄§ Lord, teach me to speak more loudly in my actions than in my words.

WISDOM LINGERS

In her *Life of Sir Richard Burton* Lady Burton made the following classification of men:

"There are four sorts of men:

> *He who knows not and knows not he knows not: he is a fool—shun him;*
>
> *He who knows not and knows he knows not: he is simple—teach him.*
>
> *He who knows and knows not he knows: he is asleep —wake him.*
>
> *He who knows and knows he knows: he is wise— follow him."*

Perhaps the hardest thing for any of us to do is to see ourselves clearly for what we are. Much of the trouble in the world comes, as a matter of natural course, from those who try to impose a false estimate of themselves on others. We cannot truly devote ourselves to others if we are not honest with ourselves first.

🙚 Lord, help me to know myself that I may better serve others.

IT ISN'T SO

At a ticket window of a roller-skating rink in a Midwest city three little girls—two white and one colored—appeared one day. They were dangling their skates over their shoulders and their faces were aglow with anticipation of the pleasures to come. The ticket agent took one look at them and proceeded to dash their hopes. *"We can't have colored children on our rink,"* he told them. *"You two"*—he indicated the white youngsters—*"can go in. Your friend will have to stay outside."*

The three girls promptly consulted among themselves. Then the two white girls bought their tickets and went inside, leaving their companion behind. About a half-hour later they were back again at the ticket booth. *"It isn't so,"* they told the startled agent. *"We asked every person on the rink and they said they'd be glad to have our friend here."* Shamefaced, the agent agreed to have the little colored girl admitted to the rink.

It is the same way with a lot of otherwise good people. There is the ever-present danger of developing prejudices by not having full possession of the facts. A Christopher, on the other hand, should go "overboard" in sharing Christ's love with all men. The very least he should do is to show the *normal* courtesies to those whom others might tend to ridicule or avoid.

"This is my commandment, that you love one another, as I have loved you." (John 13:35)

Pray that you will show love for others because of your love for Him.

A FEW COULD DO IT

"If they could have as free a hand on the job as a rocket expert has in figuring out an improved robot bomb, a hundred men could help mankind turn the world into a paradise." This startling claim, made in a brief but emphatic editorial in *This Week* magazine, struck a responsive chord in the hearts of many thinking men.

All the great trends of history, for better or worse, have been started by only a few people. A small group of human beings was able to sow the discord and destruction which we have witnessed—and still are witnessing—in our time. And almost two thousand years ago a dozen obscure fishermen, gathering around the Prince of Peace, started the greatest movement for *good* the world has ever seen.

By following the example of those first Christophers, by working out more effective ways of spreading the truths of Christ already in our hands, we yet may be able —to paraphrase the words of the magazine article—to "remake the world for peace."

"But as many as received him, he gave them power to be made the sons of God . . ." (John 1:12)

᪥ Pray always that you may do *your* part in restoring peace to the world.

THE HAPPY OUTLOOK

An old Arabian fable tells of a prince imprisoned in a castle which had thirteen windows. Twelve of these windows overlooked lovely scenes, while the thirteenth looked down on the black ash heaps of the city. Ignoring the twelve windows, the prince always looked out through the thirteenth.

It is so often true that whether a person carries with him an atmosphere of gloom and depression or one of confidence and courage depends on his individual outlook.

Of course it isn't always easy to have a cheerful attitude, yet one of the best ways to develop and maintain a reasonably happy view of life is to help those who are troubled and in despair. This is the Christopher approach. One who, with Christ's help, strives to bring light into darkness, health into the midst of disease—to the poor in body and in spirit—inevitably gains much pleasure. His attitude, instead of being morbid, is unfailingly hopeful.

"Bow down thy ear cheerfully to the poor . . . Deliver him that suffereth wrong out of the hand of the proud: and be not fainthearted in thy soul." (Ecclesiasticus 4:8–9)

❧ Lord, grant that I may develop a cheerful outlook on life by bringing cheer to others.

IT PAID DIVIDENDS

A man who spent twenty-seven years as a college professor received, not long ago, an unexpected tribute. An anonymous ex-student of his donated a $15,000 scholarship in his honor. The ex-student, a housewife and mother, wrote a heartfelt explanatory letter saying that as a result of her studies under this professor ". . . *my life has been enriched in many ways. Inner resources have been built up, friendships have been found, and, most important of all, I have been better equipped for the job of motherhood.*"

Then, after describing the teacher's fine qualities, the donor went on to say: "*It seems to me that a teacher who is able to direct the hidden springs of energy into a constructive path on the part of his students, who is able without distortion or drama to give a fuller life to the people he is guiding, is indeed a great man.*"

We can all be stimulated by the example of this teacher, who produced such a wonderful and far-reaching effect simply by doing his job well and sincerely. Through his example we can see how the world is within reach of us all.

Grant me a sense of honest craftsmanship in imitation of Christ, Who did all things well.

"WITHOUT WAX"

Many of the wealthier Romans lived in marble palaces. Often enough a piece of marble would be chipped off, spoiling the beautiful façade and, naturally, a workman would have to be called in to make repairs.

Sometimes a dishonest workman would fill in the chink with a kind of cement called wax, an imitation marble. For a while the deception would not be discovered; but after a time the wax would become discolored, revealing the defect. Hence it became necessary to put into contracts for repairs a clause stating that the work would be done *sine cera*—without wax. This, some believe, is the origin of the word *sincere*.

A life that is sincere is one which makes no pretensions, has nothing to hide.

"And this I pray, that your charity may more and more abound in knowledge, and in all understanding: That you may approve the better things, that you may be sincere and without offense unto the day of Christ . . ." (Philippians 1:9, 10)

&ecst; Grant me, O Lord, always to be sincere before God and man.

WHY SO LATE?

Just before he ascended the gallows following the Nuremberg trials, Hans Frank, one of the top Nazis who controlled Poland, made a statement. He claimed he had little idea, until it was too late, that turning away from God could have such destructive and deadly consequences.

"It was not only because of technical reasons and unfortunate coincidences that we lost the war," he said. *"It was not just ill luck and treason. Rather God has passed sentence on Hitler. He has passed it on him and his system which we served in a state of mind hostile to God."*

He then implored that everything be done to warn others not to follow in his path. *"Not even one step,"* he emphasized, since the way he followed was *"the way without God, the road from Christ, and in the final outcome the road of political stupidity, of disaster and death."*

Why do men wait until it is so late to learn the age-old lesson that defying God means bringing a piece of hell not only into their own lives but into the lives of countless others? How much wiser to remember, before it's too late, that *". . . it is impossible to escape Thy hand. For the wicked that denied to know Thee were scourged by the strength of Thy arm . . ."* (Wisdom 16:15–16)

Grant, O God, that those misled by evil may repent of their wickedness and that good men may not default by negligence.

FOUNDATIONS

A hurricane a few years ago hit Long Island with terrible force. The next morning, when the wind and the lashing rain had stopped, the inhabitants inspected the great damage.

The scene that greeted them was a dreadful and unfamiliar one. Thousands of trees had been uprooted and lay stretched on the ground and blocking roads. After their initial shock at the devastation of the landscape, the people noted that only the sturdiest trees stood. They saw those that had fallen were the rotten ones or those with shallow roots, unable to resist the storm.

"Everyone who comes to me and hears my words and acts upon them, I will show you to whom he is like:

"He is like a man building a house, who dug deep and laid a foundation upon rock. And when a flood came, the stream broke against that house and could not shake it, because it was founded on rock.

"But he who has heard my words and has not acted upon them is like a man who built his house upon the ground without a foundation; against which the stream broke and straightway it fell in, and great was the wreck of that house." (Luke 6:47–49)

⋙ Lord, help me to build my life upon Thee, the only permanent foundation.

CHAIN REACTION

In a small California town a young Negro, studying to be a teacher, took a part-time job at a filling station to help support himself and his wife until he got his degree. But some customers objected; they wanted to buy gasoline only from white men. The owner was about to fire the boy when a woman neighbor asked:

"How many customers will you lose if you stand by this man?"

"About eighteen. Maybe twenty."

"If I get you twenty new customers, you will keep him on?"

"You bet I will."

Not only did this Christopher bring twenty new customers, but five more for good measure. Her story has been told and retold to hundreds of thousands. Recently, when the *Reader's Digest* published an article on the Christophers, in which this story was included, at least fifteen million readers derived encouragement from her example.

Few stop to think of the far-reaching effects of even the simplest kindness done in the name of Christ by anyone ready to go out of his way in exercising personal responsibility for the good of others. One act of kindness performed for another may inspire thousands, even millions, to similar effort.

&§ O God, teach me at least to try to reach for the world in Thy name.

THE CHOICE IS YOURS

To those who think it is enough to know what is right and simply avoid doing anything wrong, Emerson had something important to say. In one of his essays occurs the following profound sentence:

"God offers to every mind its choice between truth and repose. Take which you please—you can never have both."

Most of us would like to disbelieve this truth: there's no denying that comfort is more pleasant than work. But we have to admit that *knowing* what is right implies the obligation to spread that knowledge.

And, as a matter of fact, many people who have fought "the good fight" with unceasing zeal testify to the rewarding satisfaction, the deep contentment that is the reward of the struggle.

"It is better to wear out than to rust out." (Richard Cumberland)

⋑ Pray for the grace to keep pushing on when it would be so easy to stop trying.

BEGIN IN TIME

The American Cancer Society in its tireless campaign to prevent cancer deaths has succeeded in bringing symptoms of the disease to public attention. Like all evils, cancer has no limits or barriers; likewise it has a tiny beginning and must be counteracted early; countless lives are wasted because it is not attended to in time. As someone observed: *"It is no disgrace to have cancer. The only disgrace is not doing something about it in time."*

Have you stopped to think how much importance we are giving to this matter of cancer, a physical defect that lasts only a lifetime? If we give so much importance to the evils that attack the body, how much more attention should we give to the spiritual evils which attack our soul and last an eternity?

Like cancer, evils which attack our spiritual beliefs begin as tiny things with unlimited aims; they must be stopped before it is too late.

◄§ Pray for the wisdom to recognize evil and the strength to resist it.

TAKE HEART!

Sometimes we let past failures discourage us from acting positively. But we have only to look at the lives of great men of the past to see how they refused to be daunted by their mistakes. Instead, they learned something from each failure and went on courageously toward success.

A typical example is Peter himself. Immediately after Our Lord made him the head of the church, Peter showed a lack of understanding of Christ's destiny and was rebuked: *"Go behind me, Satan, thou art a scandal unto me because thou savorest not the things that are of God, but the things that are of men."* (Matthew 16:23)

And yet Peter went on to become a great leader and a martyr: an example to us all. We don't have to rationalize or minimize our mistakes, but face them, learn from them, and gain strength to go on.

"We are of God. He that knows God listens to us; he who is not of God does not listen to us. In this way we know the Spirit of Truth and the spirit of error." (I John 4:6)

♫ Lord, help me to profit by my past weaknesses and mistakes.

ONE BY ONE

To most of us God gives a gentle reminder of our approaching end. One by one our hairs fall out. One by one our teeth fall out. Bit by bit our beauty fades; little by little our strength wanes; gradually our vision dims. Thus He lets us know that eternity is never very far away from any of us.

Yet many in our land and over the world somehow fail to notice these little signs of what is to come. An eternity of Heaven or Hell is in store for each of us, whether we are aware of it or not.

To those who drift through life, without thought of their destiny, each of us would show real solicitude by bringing into their lives some reminder of this tremendous truth.

By way of quiet affirmation or kindly hint we can do our part to help others prepare themselves to meet their Creator face to face.

". . . *it is appointed unto men once to die, and after this the judgment.*" (Hebrews 9:27)

O God, have mercy on all men, particularly those who are to appear before Thee this day.

A LITTLE KNOWLEDGE

A high-school girl, seated next to a famous astronomer at a dinner party, struck up a conversation with him by asking: *"What do you do for a living?"* *"I study astronomy,"* he replied. *"Really?"* said the teen-ager, wide-eyed. *"I finished astronomy last year."*

Many people stop growing mentally and spiritually at an early age. Physically, they continue to develop, but spiritually they remain as six-year-olds. Yet most of us—like the famous English writer and teacher who had the habit of listing his occupation always as "student"—do recognize that we have a lot to learn, especially in those things which concern us spiritually.

The words and actions of other people are one of the best sources of learning. By appreciating those around us, by realizing how much one can share with them and gain from them, we inevitably grow daily in knowledge and in love.

"Wisdom preacheth abroad, she uttereth her voice in the streets." (Proverbs 1:20)

O Lord, help me to grow each day in knowledge and love of others.

INSPIRED WORDS

One of the great canticles of all time is Mary's humble and joyous affirmation to Elizabeth of the divine birth as recorded in the Gospel of St. Luke.

In the light of our eternal destiny each of us can repeat her inspired words:

"My soul doth magnify the Lord.
"And my spirit hath rejoiced in God my Saviour.
"Because he hath regarded the humility of his hand-maid; for behold from henceforth all generations shall call me blessed.
"Because he that is mighty, hath done great things to me: and holy is his name.
"And his mercy is from generation unto generations, to them that fear him.
"He hath shewed might in his arm: he hath scattered the proud in the conceit of their heart.
"He hath put down the mighty from their seat, and hath exalted the humble.
"He hath filled the hungry with good things: and the rich he hath sent empty away.
"He hath received Israel his servant, being mindful of his mercy:
"As he spoke to our fathers, to Abraham and to his seed for ever." (Luke 1:46–55)

❧ Pray that you, too, may always rejoice in God your Saviour.

NOT TO THE STRONG ALONE

On the eve of the American Revolution Patrick Henry made a stirring speech before the Virginia House of Burgesses. Urging his fellow Virginians to fight, he pointed out that they had no need to fear, since they had received strength from God:

". . . I repeat it, sir, we must fight! An appeal to arms and to the God of Hosts is all that is left us! . . . Sir, we are not weak, if we make a proper use of the means which the God of nature hath placed in our power . . . Besides, sir, we shall not fight our battles alone. There is a just God who presides over the destinies of nations; and who will raise friends to fight our battles for us. The battle, sir, is not to the strong alone; it is to the vigilant, the active, the brave . . .

". . . Should I keep back my opinions at such a time, through fear of giving offense, I should consider myself as guilty of treason toward my country, and of an act of disloyalty toward the majesty of heaven, which I revere above all earthly kings."

This was the faith which sustained the men at Valley Forge. It is the only faith which can sustain us through this time of tragedy and terror.

❧ Pray that you may fear God alone and nothing else.

OUR TRUE GREATNESS

It's something more than our lofty skylines, our huge factories, our inventive genius, that makes up the greatness of our land. Deeper still is the spirit that makes it possible: the belief that every human being counts because he is made in the image of God. Into our Declaration of Independence we put our conviction that *"all men . . . are endowed by their Creator with certain unalienable rights."*

This isn't a "made-in-America" proposition. We have no monopoly on it—this conviction belongs to the world. If ours is the world vision of Christ, we will never be satisfied to keep this fundamental to ourselves. We will want to spread it to all men.

"Have you nothing better to offer us than machines?" asked an outstanding Hindu not long ago. *"Has Western civilization no other gifts for us save the electric dynamo, the motorcar, the locomotive, and the machine gun? We can get along without these, but we do need ideas that can benefit our people. . . ."*

"In every nation he that feareth God and worketh justice is acceptable to him." (Acts 10:35)

&§ O Lord, teach me ever to keep a clear vision of the spiritual basis of our nation.

185

THE GREATER FOOL

An English nobleman gave a jester a wand, saying: *"Keep this until you find a greater fool than yourself."* The jester laughingly accepted the wand and flourished it on festive occasions.

One day the nobleman lay dying. Calling the jester to his bedside, he said: *"I am going on a long journey."* *"Where to?"* asked the jester. *"I don't know,"* came the reply. *"How long will you be gone?"* asked the jester. *"I shall be gone forever,"* came the reply. *"What provisions have you made for the trip?"* the jester asked. The nobleman shrugged his shoulders. *"None at all."*

"Then," said the jester, *"take this."* And placing the wand in the nobleman's hands, he added: *"It belongs to you."*

Those who fail to realize the purpose of life—where they came from and where they are going—are running a foolish risk. You can help them out of their predicament by praying for them and by "going" to them with the love that Christ has given to you.

"The fool hath said in his heart: There is no God. They are corrupt, and are become abominable in their ways: there is none that doth good, no not one." (Psalm 13:1)

⋙ Lord, let me not fail to make provision for the long journey.

FACE THE FACTS

Some time ago a Minneapolis woman gave her life's savings to a persuasive crook when she was assured the money would be profitably invested in a legitimate business concern. Naturally, the swindler skipped town and left no trace of his whereabouts. When the woman reported the case to the city's Better Business Bureau, one of the Bureau officials interrupted her tale of woe with this question: *"Why didn't you come to us first? Obviously you knew about our service."*

"Yes, I knew all right," was the astonishing answer, *"but I was afraid if I told you what I intended to do, you'd tell me not to do it!"*

Everywhere it's the same old story. People refuse to face facts because they are afraid that knowledge of the truth will make demands upon them. Yet a moment of serious reflection should convince them that it is the truth which protects them and saves them from the misery of disillusionment.

"And you shall know the truth, and the truth shall make you free." (John 8:32)

❧ Pray for a courageous love of truth.

"WHAT WILT THOU HAVE ME TO DO?"

One of the greatest examples in history of how love can effect a full and speedy transformation is that of St. Paul. Christ's loving solicitude accounts for the sudden change of Paul from a persecutor into the most docile and willing worker for His cause. As the Scriptures tell us:

"In those days, Saul, as yet breathing out threatenings and slaughter against the disciples of the Lord, went to the high priest,

"And asked of him letters to Damascus, to the synagogues: that if he found any men and women of this way, he might bring them bound to Jerusalem.

"And as he went on his journey, it came to pass that he drew nigh to Damascus: and suddenly a light from heaven shined round about him.

"And falling on the ground, he heard a voice saying to him: Saul, Saul, why persecutest thou Me! *Who said:* Who art Thou, Lord? *And He said:* I am Jesus of Nazareth, whom thou persecutest. It is hard for thee to kick against the goad.

"And he trembling and astonished, said: Lord, what wilt Thou have me to do? *And the Lord said to him:* Arise, and go into the city, and there it shall be told thee what thou must do."

Among those who seem to be our enemies are many potential Christophers. Yet, they often turn quickly to the very Cause they revile. Love alone prepares the way for this.

⋙ O Jesus, inspire me with the same confidence in Thee that Thy Apostle Paul displayed when he asked: *"Lord, what wilt Thou have me to do?"* (Acts 9:6)

PUT THE MAN RIGHT

An overworked businessman came home one night, hoping to read the evening paper in peace and quiet. But his six-year-old son wanted attention. Tearing into small pieces a part of the paper which had a map of the world on one side of it and the picture of a man on the other, the father gave it to his son and told him to put the map back together again.

In ten minutes his son returned, the task completed. Since the boy had no idea of geography, the businessman wondered how he had done so well. *"All I did,"* said the boy, *"was to put the man right. When I did that, the world came out right!"*

The big battle of our day is over man—*the worth of man.* It is a battle for man's soul. Are you doing as much to reach all men with the truth of their divine origin as are those who deny God and are striving to eliminate all knowledge of Him from the face of the earth?

"Our wrestling is not against flesh and blood; but against . . . the world-rulers of this darkness. (Ephesians 6:12)

⋅᧗ Lord, help me to do my part in the battle for man's soul.

SECOND CHANCE

In the Academy at Florence one of the great Italian masterpieces displayed is Michelangelo's statue *"David."* Yearly thousands of people admire this early example of the great master's work, unaware that the huge block of stone from which the figure was hewn has a curious history.

At first, an inferior artist began to work on it, but through lack of skill, he succeeded only in hacking and marring the marble. Then the rulers of Florence called on the young Michelangelo, who created a lasting work of art.

There is no one so ruined that he is undeserving of a second chance. As the true artist saw in the shapeless mass of stone the outline of his masterpiece, so God sees in the lowest of the low that unextinguished spark of goodness and humanity which can be his salvation.

All of us can do the same, looking at everyone in a creative, not destructive, spirit. God will guide us in the good work of restoring what was lost, of giving life to what was spiritually dead.

"The son of man is come to save that which was lost." (Matthew 18:11)

O Lord as you have so often given me a second chance, grant that I may always help others to have their second chance.

IN THE NAME OF CHARITY

In a certain town a campaign to promote brotherhood was underway, and at one of the public meetings a prominent citizen had the floor.

"I'd like to take these people who are spreading enmity among us," he shouted during the course of his remarks, *"and put them in front of a firing squad!"*

The Devil slows down and even wrecks many a fine work dedicated to the common good by stirring up stupid hostilities and antagonisms.

Paradoxically enough, too often it is those who complain most of bitterness who are even more hateful themselves, thereby scandalizing many and hurting a cause much more than they help it. In the name of charity, they make bad into worse, by gossip, by self-righteous condemnations, and by other moves that enlarge the wound rather than heal it.

"If any man say, I love God and hateth his brother, he is a liar. For he that loveth not his brother whom he seeth, how can he love God Whom he seeth not?" (John 1:4, 20)

✍ Say a fervent prayer for those who mistakenly think they can love God while they still show bitterness to others.

A GOOD DISPOSITION

Some time ago we took a ride on a New York bus. There was nothing exceptional about the trip except the driver of the bus, who was remarkable for his patience and cheerfulness.

We watched him through the course of the trip, as he called out the streets, made change, issued transfers. His composure was unruffled even by those who asked annoying questions or made irritable comments. At ease himself, he seemed to be able to put everyone else at his ease.

Actually, a good disposition causes less wear and tear on the human frame than a bad disposition does. A scientist pointed out once that a smile involves the use of twelve facial muscles, whereas a frown takes nearly five times as many. So a pleasant outlook not only works wonders with others, but is easier—and better for you in the long run.

"Wherefore, sirs, be of good cheer; for I believe God that it shall so be, as it hath been told me." (Acts 27:25)

Lord, teach me to be ever patient and cheerful that I may become an example encouraging to others.

JUST AS EASY

A child who had spent quite a bit of extra time at her prayers one evening, and had been questioned by her mother as to the reason, replied: *"I was praying that all bad people would be good and all good people nice!"*

One of the greatest injuries to religion comes from a few of its most loyal adherents who are correct in all matters *save one*. They persist in being disagreeable when it would be just as easy to remain agreeable, even while differing with others.

If they realized how that slightly sour note has a big effect in keeping large numbers away from religion, many would undoubtedly change to a more pleasant attitude without delay. It is most important for a Christopher to be *pleasantly* firm when it is necessary to be firm. But being disagreeable is a sign of weakness.

"He that saith he is in the light, and hateth his brother, is in darkness even until now. He that loveth his brother, abideth in the light, and there is no scandal in him." (I John 2: 9–10)

⊸§ Lord, help me always to be kind.

WASHINGTON PITCHED IN

In the Revolutionary War, during preparations for a battle, a man in civilian clothes passed a corporal who was arrogantly ordering his men to lift a heavy beam. The man stopped and asked the corporal, *"Why don't you help them?"* *"Sir,"* the answer came back indignantly. *"I am a corporal!"*

With a muttered apology, the stranger stripped off his coat and pitched in to help the soldiers. *"Mr. Corporal,"* he said when the task was done, *"whenever you haven't enough men to do a job, call on your commander in chief. I'll be glad to help."* With that, George Washington put on his coat and left.

To help others we must often humble ourselves; but, paradoxically enough, we always win by doing so. The best proof of this is Christ himself. He became the friend and servant of the lowest among men, lepers and beggars and thieves. And for this all mankind reveres Him.

"He that is greatest among you shall be your servant." (Matthew 23:11)

&ed; Lord, help me to remember that in the measure that I humble myself, in Your name, for others, You will exalt me in Your presence.

DO IT!

There are various ways by which a Christopher can pass on to others the principles that guide his life and give it eternal purpose. The following ways are suggested as the most practical and, it is felt, offer the best chance of producing lasting results:

1. *By listening to those in trouble.* Many who are confused, in sorrow, in doubt, or discouraged want to talk to someone. That may be the very moment in their lives when they will listen to the real Truth. A kind word, a helping hand, listening to those in trouble may often be the means of bringing the peace of Christ into their lives.

2. *By interest in evildoers.* The very purpose of Christ's coming to earth was to win sinners. He asked those who would be Christophers to do the same. Rather than devote attention to "saving the saved," one of the Christopher's chief objectives should be to reach those who are farthest from Christ and therefore need Him most. It is easy to talk to those who agree with us, but to hold the attention of those opposed or indifferent is the real job of the bearer of Christ.

"That you may be the children of your Father who is in heaven, who maketh his sun to rise upon the good, and bad, and raineth upon the just and the unjust." (Matthew 5:45)

"Be not overcome by evil, but overcome evil by good." (Romans 12:21)

(continued tomorrow)

❧ Lord, help me to love those whom it is difficult to like.

DO IT! (continued)

3. *By informing those who know not.* Most of the hundred million in our country who are not reached by anyone in the name of Christ actually hunger for His teachings. Too few Christians are interested in them, as well as in the billion and more in paganism over the world. Many who have no religion feel that Christianity does not want them, because it makes so little attempt to reach them. A Christopher should bear in mind the words of Paul to the Romans:

". . . Or how shall they believe him of whom they have not heard? And how shall they hear, without a preacher?" (Romans 10:14)

4. *By taking part in public life.* This is the strict duty of all citizens. Men have a special responsibility, but women have an important role also. Only recently Pope Pius XII made an emphatic statement about women's role in public life:

"The fate of the family, the fate of human relations are at stake. They are in your hands. Every woman has then . . . the strict obligation in conscience . . . to go into action in a . . . way suitable to the condition of each, so as to hold back those currents which threaten the home, so as to oppose those doctrines which undermine its foundations, so as to prepare, organize, and achieve its restoration."

≈§ Pray that in large numbers Christophers will bring Christ to those who know Him not.

SPARK OF GENIUS

A gifted artist, walking in the countryside, saw a small boy painting on a flat rock, while his sheep browsed nearby. The boy was using cheap colors and a homemade brush yet his painting showed unmistakable talent. The artist took the boy under his wing, fostered and taught him. The spark of genius burst into a flame and the boy became one of the world's most renowned painters.

We often hear people complain, *"If only I were talented!" "How I would love to play the piano!" "I wish I had his abilities!"* and so on. And they waste their lives in useless wishing, envy, and self-frustration. Yet actually they may possess the talent they envy in others.

Potentiality is never known except in action. If we would only make a start, we might find we had the potentiality. And if we continue to act, often we will *build up* the ability we desire.

"Ask, and it shall be given you; seek, and you shall find; knock, and it shall be opened to you." (Matthew 7:7)

❧ Lord, whatever I do, give me the spirit to do it well.

DAY OF RECKONING

The end of the world seems far off, so most of us don't bother to think about it. Yet Christ repeatedly referred to it, and certainly we can better our lives if we think of our last end. In a striking parable Jesus described the Last Judgment:

"And the servants of the good man of the house coming said to him: Sir, didst thou not sow good seed in thy field? whence then hath it cockle? And he said to them: An enemy hath done this. And the servants said to him: Wilt thou that we go and gather it up?

"And he said to them: No, lest perhaps gathering up the cockle, you root up the wheat also together with it.

"Suffer both to grow until the harvest, and in the time of the harvest I will say to the reapers: Gather up first the cockle, and bind it into bundles to burn, but the wheat gather ye into my barn. So shall it be at the end of the world. The angels shall go out, and shall separate the wicked from among the just.

"And shall cast them into the furnace of fire: there shall be weeping and gnashing of teeth." (Matthew 13: 27-30; 49-50)

≼§ Lord, help me to remember that Thou wilt judge me.

MY HANDS . . . AND MY GOD

A poor woman was abandoned by her husband and left with no visible means of support. When the case came up in court, the judge asked the wife: *"Madam, have you any means of support whatever?"*

"Well, your honor," she answered, *"I have three, to tell the truth."*

"Three!"

"Yes, sir."

"What are they?" asked the astonished judge.

"My hands, my good health, and my God, your honor," came back the reply.

The resourcefulness of this woman, her self-reliance, and her dependence upon God, can be a lesson to all of us. The old saying *"God helps those who help themselves"* is still valid. The strength we derive from our faith in God gives us the courage to have confidence in ourselves.

"Our God is our refuge and strength; a helper in troubles, which have found us exceedingly." (Psalms 45:4)

Lord, Thou art my hope; be my strength.

DROP YOUR BUCKETS

An ocean vessel, limping in from the sea, dropped anchor at some distance from the mouth of a river and signaled to the shore for fresh water. Back came the answer, *"Drop your buckets!"*

The captain became angry, thinking it hardly the time or place for a joke. Again he signaled for water, adding, *"Let's be serious about this."*

Again came the answer: *"Drop your buckets."*

For the third time the captain signaled. When he received the same answer the third time, he ordered the buckets dipped into the water. When they were pulled up, the water was found to be fresh.

We often think that the real opportunities to develop our character, to do something big, lie far off. Actually, we need only dip our bucket into the flowing river of everyday life to find ample opportunity for service to Our Lord.

". . . but at Thy word I will let down the net." (Luke 5:5)

Lord, help me to see my opportunities for service to Thee in my daily round of duty.

200

GIVE CREDIT WHERE IT IS DUE

Two men were discussing their respective accomplishments, and during the conversation one of them proudly announced: *"Everything I am I owe to myself. I'm a self-made man!"*

It is symptomatic of a lack of insight when we make the mistake of thinking we are "self-made." Our bodies and brains we receive from God through our parents. Our knowledge we acquire from those who have gone before us. Many of our skills depend upon our physical make-up. Our tastes and appreciations have come to us through our association with those who love the finer things. Even that very precious possession, our conscience, will be affected for good or ill according to the training we receive. It is not a mysterious something requiring no guidance or training.

So there it is: our bodies, temperaments, brains we receive at birth. Other people pass on to us the accumulated culture of the race. We know right from wrong largely because we have been told which is which. Why, then, should we flatter ourselves that everything we have and are is our own masterpiece? Let's give credit where it is due. As St. Paul said,

". . . what hast thou that thou hast not received? And if thou hast received, why dost thou glory, as if thou hadst not received it?" (I Corinthians 4:7)

◦§ Lord, let me be humbly grateful and intelligently humble at the thought of all I have been given by Thee.

PLAYING IT TOO SAFE

A farmer was sitting on his porch, glumly staring into space, when a passer-by called to him: *"How's your cotton this year?"*

"Ain't got none," answered the farmer. *"Afraid of boll weevils."*

"What about your corn?"

"Season looked dry so I didn't plant none."

The stranger was puzzled. *"What did you plant?"*

"Nuthin," said the farmer. *"I played it safe."*

There are a lot of us who *"play it safe"* by doing nothing with our talents, by burying them and feeling righteous about it, while we watch others expose themselves to risk and failure. But if we take the example of Christ and His apostles, we can see the error of false security. We can be safe only when we are acting boldly for Christ.

"In this is my Father glorified: that you bring forth very much fruit, and become my disciples." (John 15:8)

∾ Inspire me, O God, to will and to accomplish something in Thy name.

BORN TO LABOR

Not long ago there was a serious shortage of nurses for the necessary routine work in hospitals. A newspaper editorial pointed out that an increasing number of nurses was finding it difficult to pass up attractive positions *"as private nurses in the homes of well-to-do semi-invalids, where the food and surroundings are of a high quality, the hours short, the salaries usually above even the maximum standard paid by voluntary hospitals . . ."*

It is human nature to do as little work as possible and expect as much as possible for it. But most happiness in this life (as well as the next) comes as the result of hard work. And the magic ingredient which turns any work from drudgery into joy is the amount of ourselves that we put into it.

"Man is born to labor and the bird to fly." (Job 5:7)

Lord, let me put my heart into my work as a work done for Thee.

"TALK AND DO"

A frequent inmate of the county jail in a small Midwest community has for his motto *"Death before dishonor."* Writing it down on a piece of paper, however, wasn't enough for him. He had it tattooed on his arm! To him can be applied the question often on the lips of a skeptic: *"Do you talk and do, or do you only talk?"*

This danger has been eloquently expressed by C. S. Lewis's devil in *The Screwtape Letters,* as he refers to his effort to tempt the good man: *"The great thing is to prevent his doing anything. As long as he does not convert it into action, it does not matter how much he thinks about this new repentance. Let the brute wallow in it.... The more often he feels without acting, the less he will ever be able to act, and, in the long run, the less he will be able to feel."*

Talk without performance is evidence of lack of sincerity. One of the easiest ways to *be* good is to *do* good.

"Even as the body without the spirit is dead, so also faith without good works is dead." (James 2:26)

⋙ Jesus, Who went about doing good, inspire me to imitate You.

ALL IN THE POINT OF VIEW!

An anonymous author has given expression to a valuable thought which calls for no comment from us:

"When the other fellow acts that way, he's *ugly*;
"When you do it, it's *nerves*.
"When he's set in his ways, he's *obstinate*;
"When you are, it's just *firmness*.
"When he doesn't like your friends, he's *prejudiced*;
"When you don't like his, you are simply *showing good judgment of human nature*.
"When he tries to be accommodating, he's *polishing the apple*;
"When you do it, you're using *tact*.
"When he takes time to do things, he is *dead slow*;
"When you take ages, you are *deliberate*.
"When he picks flaws, he's *cranky*;
"When you do, you're *discriminating*."

"*With what judgment you judge, you shall be judged, and with what measure you mete, it shall be measured to you again.*" (Matthew 7:2)

❧ Pray for the grace to see your own faults before you look for faults in others.

"SON OF THUNDER"

So impetuous was the Apostle James in his zeal for Christ, and so severe in temper, that he was nicknamed "Son of Thunder." He it was who wanted to call down fire from heaven upon the Samaritans who refused to receive Christ.

In A.D. 44 James suffered martyrdom for His master. An old tradition, traced to Clement of Alexandria, has it that James's accuser was so moved by the Apostle's fearless confession of Jesus Crucified that *"he declared himself a Christian on the spot,"* and both *"were hurried off together to the place of execution."* There, after begging the Apostle to forgive him, accuser and accused embraced with the words, *"Peace be with thee,"* and—as the account concludes: *"Together, then, they knelt for the sword, and together received the crown."*

"And Jesus answering, said: You know not what you ask. Can you drink the chalice that I shall drink? They say to him: We can." (Matthew 20:22)

◆§ Pray for the grace to accept suffering for His sake, and to bear it patiently and with courage.

THE STUFF OF HEROES

"*. . . Now I am a soldier in the most fascinating branch of the service there is,*" wrote Joyce Kilmer from the Western Front in 1918. And he added that he was living a "*wonderful life*"; that his was "*the finest job in the army.*"

What was the job which so captured Kilmer's admiration?

It was prowling about the woods, locating the exact position of the machine-gun nests of the enemy!

Joyce Kilmer was able to see in his dangerous—and ultimately fatal—assignment something exhilarating because he had learned to see the beautiful and the good in the trials and tribulations of life. Yet such an outlook can certainly become inadequate and superficial for us unless we learn—as Kilmer did—to associate our sufferings with the sufferings of Christ. In this lies the secret of all real courage. And it is a secret anyone may share if he will. As Our Lord Himself said:

"*Let not your heart be troubled. You believe in God, believe also in me.*" (John 14:1)

◄§ Jesus, permit me to do all things for **Thee**.

TALK DOESN'T CATCH FISH

The tremendous challenge of our times demands more than understanding and sympathy, more than token performance. The Prince of Peace bids us not to cease our efforts until we have brought His sublime message to *"all men of all nations."*

The Christopher object, therefore, is to develop a sense of personal responsibility and initiative in bringing back into the mainstream of life the major truths which alone guarantee peace for all mankind. The achievements of tens of thousands who have already gone as Christ-bearers into the four fields of influence are inspiring hope for the peaceful transformation that will take place when their number reaches a million.

Each Christopher carries Christ with him, individually and personally, into the dust and heat of the market place, thereby helping to change for the better the trends abroad in the world today. Each Christopher knows he is called by Christ Himself to be a *"fisher of men."* But he knows also that the best fisherman in the world cannot catch a single fish if he is two miles away from the water, just talking about fish.

". . . I will make you to be fishers of men." (Matthew 4:19)

&ξ O Lord, teach me to realize that You are with me always.

NAPOLEON IN THE COUNTINGHOUSE

"Since aptitudes may remain dormant and undeveloped," said an industrial psychologist not long ago, *"a man may not even know that he possesses them . . .*

"Many a Napoleon has remained a clerk . . . in a countinghouse without even dreaming that he might have been a great general. Many a man capable of breaking the world's record in the quarter-mile dash has never ventured on a cinder track. Many a skilled mechanic has remained a common laborer because circumstances never arose which permitted him to discover the aptitude and develop it into an ability."

How true it is that many never discover their talents! One of the ways in which we can help in spreading Christ's truth to all men is by ferreting out talent. We can help others to see that they have abilities which could be used for good purposes. Our Lord gave us an example to follow when He told His listeners, *"You are the light of the world . . ."* (Matthew 5:14)

O God, allow me to assist others in discovering their power for good.

DANGER OF COMPROMISING

A cartoon in a national humor magazine recently amused us very much. The drawing showed a self-satis-fied-looking gentleman and his wife leaving church on a bright Sunday morning.

"Everything considered," the gentleman was declaring, *"he preaches remarkably good sermons. It's so hard to avoid offending people like us."*

While it is true that *"honey catches more flies than vinegar,"* we should, at all costs, avoid making compromises with what we believe to be right. In the long run people will respect us more for dignified disagreement with them than for any kind of fawning agreement.

"If then you fulfill the royal law, according to the scriptures, Thou shalt love thy neighbour as thyself; you do well. But if you have respect to persons, you commit sin, being reproved by the law as transgressors." (James 2:8–9)

⋙ Lord, let me not be too weak to respect my own point of view or so obstinate as to belittle that of others.

TO THE "BLIND"

During an annual drive in New York for contributions for the blind, store windows on Fifth Avenue were ablaze with posters. But there was one sign—a very simple one—that seemed to arrest most of the passers-by. It read:

"You can see. Will you help those who cannot?"

There is no one of us who would not, if it were in his power, restore a blind man's sight. Yet each of us must know many people who are spiritually blinded by prejudice, hatred, or ignorance. They need our help, and we can give it. Even if our own spiritual sight is not yet perfect, we can still lead those others toward the eternal light.

"Which Jesus knowing, saith to them: Why do you reason, because you have no bread? do you not yet know nor understand? have you still your heart blinded? Having eyes, see you not? and having ears, hear you not? neither do you remember." (Mark 8:17–18)

⊷ Grant, O Lord, that as we have been enabled by Thy grace to see Thy beauty and Thy truth, so may we help those who cannot see.

START WITH YOURSELF

Ignatius Loyola once wrote: *"The man who sets about making others better is wasting his time, unless he begins with himself."* This does not mean, of course, that one has to be perfect in all things before he tries to help others. But it does mean that you should acknowledge your own faults and strive to correct them even while you try to do your part in winning the world back to Christ.

"And why seest thou the mote that is in thy brother's eye; and seest not the beam that is in thy own eye?

"Or, how sayest thou to thy brother: Let me cast the mote out of thy eye; and behold a beam is in thy own eye?

"Thou hypocrite, cast out first the beam out of thy own eye, and then shalt thou see to cast out the mote out of thy brother's eye." (Matthew 7:3–5)

◆§ O Lord, help me to begin making others better by starting with myself; but help me to remember that though I start with myself I must not finish there.

STARTLING ABSENCE

In a recent letter to the New York *Herald Tribune*, commenting on the lack of a dependence upon God in the management of states and nations, a captain in the United States Naval Reserve offered these penetrating observations on a situation too little recognized today:

"*. . . In Washington, in Paris, in Moscow, in any of the centers where representatives of the nations gather to seek concord out of the chaos of the world, there is a startling absence of recognition of the part which could be played by the Creator of the world if He was asked to assist in solving its problems.*

"*Americans continue to display the slogan, 'In God We Trust,' but in practice they become too absorbed . . . to apply the principle they are expounding.*

"*As a Nation there is grave danger that we are . . . seeking by human effort alone to solve the world's ills. . . .*"

The timeliness of the thoughts here expressed calls to mind the remark of a man who knew his own limitations and the infinite resourcefulness of God. As he put it: "*When I pray, I pray as if everything depended upon God. And when I work, I work as if everything depended upon myself.*" Exactly the spirit of every real Christopher!

"*The beginning of the pride of man is to fall off from God.*" (Ecclesiasticus 10:14)

ᴥ O Lord, I place all my trust in Thee.

AT THE COST OF OTHERS

An ancient anecdote about Mohammed illustrates an important rule of conduct: that we should not try to advance ourselves by deprecating others. The story goes like this:

A disciple came to Mohammed one morning and said, *"Master, my six brothers are all asleep and I alone have remained awake to worship Allah."*

Mohammed answered him: *"And you had better been asleep, if your worship of Allah consists of accusations against your brothers."*

Faultfinding and magnifying the mistakes of others are poor ways of changing the world for the better. Wrongdoing, of course, has to be identified, but means to correct it should always be positive and constructive, not negative and destructive.

A Christopher—a bearer of Christ—will detest the sin but not the sinner. He will advance the cause of justice and peace and truth, yet he will not do so at the expense of the feelings of others. Always his motto will be: *"Better to light one candle than to curse the darkness."*

"If any man say, I love God, and hateth his brother: he is a liar. For he that loveth not his brother, whom he seeth, how can he love God, whom he seeth not?" (John 4:20)

≈§ Guide me, O Lord, that I may never strive to rise by pushing others down.

MORE THAN THE USUAL SHARE

It cannot be repeated too often that playing the role of a Christopher frequently involves more than the usual share of life's trials and difficulties. As Christ Himself said:

"Behold, I send you as sheep in the midst of wolves. Be ye therefore wise as serpents and simple as doves.

"But beware of men, for they will deliver you up in councils, and they will scourge you in their synagogues.

"And you shall be brought before governors, and before kings for my sake, for a testimony to them and to the Gentiles:

"But when they shall deliver you up, take no thought how or what to speak: for it shall be given you in that hour what to speak.

"For it is not you that speak, but the Spirit of your Father that speaketh in you.

"The brother also shall deliver up the brother to death, and the father the son: and the children shall rise up against their parents, and shall put them to death.

"And you shall be hated by all men for my name's sake: but he that shall persevere unto the end, he shall be saved." (Matthew 10: 16–22)

In the above Gospel narrative note particularly the words: *"For it is not you that speak, but the Spirit of your Father that speaketh in you."* In this fact, so clearly expressed, lies the great consolation for true bearers of Christ.

⊸§ O God, teach me to love even in the midst of hatred and suffering.

215

AN IMPORTANT DISTINCTION

As the doctor is deeply interested in his patient, regardless of how repulsive the disease, so should everyone playing the role of a Christopher show particular solicitude for anyone and everyone no matter how hostile to God that person may be.

It is most important, for example, to distinguish between Communism and the Communist. Each of us has a special obligation to love the Communist, to try, by prayer and work, to supply what is lacking in him, however much we deplore his hatred of God. We must never forget that he, too, is *made in the image and likeness of God.*

Strive to bring light to all as God "... *maketh his sun to rise upon the good and bad, and raineth upon the just and the unjust.*" (Matthew 5:45)

By a sympathetic, friendly, but firm approach, it is often possible to draw the individual Communist toward his Maker. Little, if anything, is gained by hurting, belittling, or antagonizing. Without compromising, under most circumstances it is possible—and far better—to disagree without being disagreeable.

"But I say to you, Love your enemies: do good to them that hate you: and pray for them that persecute and calumniate you." (Matthew 5:44)

Help me, Lord, to bring others to Thee through kindness.

WILLIAM PENN'S WARNING

More than two hundred and fifty years ago, when the charter of the Commonwealth of Pennsylvania was being written, William Penn, the Quaker, sounded a warning which, for our day, has a far greater significance:

"Those people who are not governed by God will be ruled by tyrants."

There is no time to lose. Not only have the great majority forgotten this fundamental fact but, still worse, millions of our young people are slowly but surely being conditioned to the Marx-Hitler dogma, that the state is the only God. It took Hitler only twelve years to sink that concept into the minds of German youth. He knew full well this was a necessary prelude to the fulfillment of the frightful orgy of death and destruction he was about to launch.

Each of us, individually and personally, can—*and must*—keep the basic truth of man's God-given rights alive by seeing to it that, at all times and in all places, it is both taught and lived.

"Thou shalt love the Lord thy God with thy whole heart, and with thy whole soul, and with thy whole mind." (Matthew 22:37)

⋖§ Beseech God in your own words to bless those who suffer under despots' rule.

THEY HAVE VISION

The paradox of the whole world situation today is that the subversive forces are doing many things for a wrong motive that we should be doing for the right one. Many of their demands on behalf of the people are the very things that Christ wanted for all human beings. They talk the language people understand. They mingle with the people. They are everlastingly on the job. They use every possible medium—press, movies, radio, comic strips, magazines, books, government, schools, labor—to further their evil ambitions. They make it a point not simply to take jobs in these key fields, but to strive for key jobs in key fields.

This dynamism, this determination to capture the world, explains why they are sweeping ever onward today while the forces of Christ lag far behind.

They have silenced forever any rationalizing that it is too hard to reach "all men," that it takes centuries to progress, that we must be content. They have shown us what can be accomplished by a small minority when organized and stimulated to action by a world vision.

◈§ Take me, O Lord, as I am, and use me as Thou wilt.

THE COST OF CONVICTION

One of the great Gospel passages is that which tells of the beheading of John the Baptist. In it there is a depth of meaning for every Christopher. It is a powerful reminder of the price one must be ready to pay for the courage of one's convictions.

The narrative begins with John's rebuke to Herod that it was not lawful for him to have his brother's wife, Herodias. And Herod, because he knew John to be a just and holy man, fearing him, listened to the rebuke. Later, at a feast, the daughter of Herodias performed a dance before the King; and Herod was so enraptured he told her: *"Whatsoever thou shalt ask I will give thee, though it be half of my kingdom."* The girl immediately asked her mother what she should request. Rankled by John's criticism and anxious to be rid of him, Herodias answered: *"The head of John the Baptist."* And then, as the Gospel continues:

"And the king was struck sad. Yet because of his oath, and because of them that were with him at table, he would not displease her:

"But sending an executioner, he commanded that his head should be brought in a dish.

"And he beheaded him in the prison, and brought his head in a dish: and gave it to the damsel, and the damsel gave it to her mother."

⋙ Pray that you will never compromise nor water down your faith but rather will die, if need be, in order to be loyal to Christ.

THE OBLIGATION TO OFFER

Christ did not ask the impossible when He commanded: *"Go ye into the whole world and preach the gospel to every creature."* (Mark 16:15)

It would be lack of faith in Him, even denial of Christ, to believe that. Since the task can be done, it should be done. Christ said definitely and precisely that we have a serious obligation to offer His blessings *"to all men."*

If some reject them, that is their responsibility. But they have the God-given right of at least learning what the teachings of their Saviour are.

The salvation of the world, of mankind itself, is dependent upon Christians co-operating with that sacred injunction: *"I have appointed thee to be a light for the Gentiles, that thou mayst bring salvation to the ends of the earth."* (Acts 13:47)

◆§ Pray that you may fulfill your privilege of helping, in however small a way, *"to bring salvation to the ends of the earth."*

SAVING FOR WHAT?

A man was walking down a dark alley, thinking his own thoughts, so he didn't notice the approach of a hold-up man until he felt a gun in his back and heard a low voice whispering: *"Your money or your life."*

"Take my life," the victim replied promptly, *"I'm saving my money for my old age."*

Some of us not only save our money for our old age, but seem to save our lives for our old age as well. We are reluctant to give ourselves to living, to dedicate our time and our spirit to a full life of the spirit, a life that concerns itself with our neighbor, whether he is next door or half a world away. Yet the truth is that only through this whole-hearted living do we really live at all.

"But lay up to yourselves treasures in heaven . . ."
(Matthew 6:20)

◦§ Lord, help me to "wear out" in Thy service instead of "rusting out" in self-preservation.

THE DEVIL'S WAY

A friend who has had considerable difficulty keeping a very worthy organization alive claims that most of the trouble comes from *within*, not from without. It is well summarized in the following ten-point satire:

1. Don't come to the meetings.

2. If you do come, come late.

3. If the weather doesn't suit you, don't come.

4. If you attend a meeting, find fault with the work of the officers and other members.

5. Never accept an office, as it is easier to criticize than to do things.

6. Feel hurt if you are not appointed to a committee, but if you are, do not attend committee meetings.

7. If asked by the chairman to give your opinion on some matter, tell him you have nothing to say. After the meeting, tell everyone how things ought to have been done.

8. Do nothing more than is absolutely necessary, but, when members roll up their sleeves and willingly, unselfishly use their ability to help matters along, say that the board is run by a clique.

9. Hold back your dues as long as possible, or don't pay them at all.

10. Don't bother about getting new members. Let someone else do it.

"Cast out the scoffer and contention shall go out with him, and quarrels and reproaches shall cease." (Proverbs 22:10)

 Pray that you will be honest in your judgment of yourself and generous in your judgment of others.

PURPOSE MAKES THE DIFFERENCE

A United States Army officer, visiting a leper colony in China, noticed an American nun dressing a leper's sores. The sight both nauseated and impressed him. Turning to the nun, he exclaimed: *"How can you do that, Sister? I wouldn't do it for a thousand dollars."*

"Well, I wouldn't do it for ten thousand!" she said calmly. Then, holding out the Crucifix of her Rosary, she added: *"But I would do it for Him."*

It is interesting to see what most of us will do once we have our vision clear. When we have seen our eternal destiny as our life's objective, sacrifice for this objective becomes comparatively easy. And the burden is not heavy —loving others for the love of God—even to the lowliest of men, because in everyone, even the poor leper, we can see Christ Himself.

"I was hungry, and you gave me to eat; I was thirsty, and you gave me to drink." (Matthew 25:35)

❧ O God, have mercy on those also who are leprous of soul.

223

ON THE MARCH

Among the Communist following, whether full-fledged members or merely sympathizers, there are few who do not possess a relentless drive to achieve their objectives. Many contributing causes might be cited, but oddly enough the ones that account most for this fanatical ardor are the techniques they have borrowed from Christianity.

After studying the Church extensively, they claimed that when its missionary, worldwide objectives, became secondary, it began to decline. That the Communists fear this for themselves is evident from their slogan: *"We must march, march, march! Once we stop marching, we decay!"*

To their followers they stress unceasingly that there is a *world* to be won, that there must be no letup, that they are the only champions of the rights of the people. They have developed a sense of sacrifice for their own cause that few Christians practice.

Not until the *believers* in Christ realize that they must be *bearers* of Christ as well, with the same flaming faith and the daring vision and sacrifice, will the forward march of the Communists be slowed to a halt and dispersed.

Pray that many will remember there is a world to be won for the peace and justice of Christ.

ON THE ALERT

In any well-disciplined army particular attention is given to the system of sentinels and guards. Any stranger approaching camp is challenged and made to identify himself. This is the case not only near the front line, but even in base areas distant from any actual fighting.

To the unthinking soldier such insistence might seem foolish, but in actuality it is just the opposite. A good soldier, engaged in a life-and-death struggle, must develop the *habit* of wariness; he must learn always to be on the watch for the enemy.

Many of us think of evil as something obvious, wearing a big label and hence easily avoided. But the forces of evil are a clever enemy, full of disguises, ready at all times to penetrate our defenses if we once relax. The true bearer of Christ is always on the alert, his eye and ear prepared to catch the first sign of the enemy's advance.

"Watch ye, therefore, praying at all times . . ." (Luke 21:36)

❧ Pray that you may always be alert to your spiritual dangers.

A POOR ALTERNATIVE

During a treason trial in Washington recently a German actor, an ex-Nazi, was called to the witness stand. When asked to take the oath, however, he announced that he was an agnostic and did not believe in reward and punishment after death.

At once the court questioned whether or not this man could testify, since our whole system of justice is based on the assumption that men believe in God. But since the testimony of this witness was so valuable, an old law stating that an unbeliever could "affirm" instead of taking the usual oath was unearthed, and on this basis the witness's testimony was heard.

That the court should be compelled to accept such an alternative reveals a dangerous trend. Surely the affirmation of those who deny the Truth is of little value. God is the foundation and source of all justice. How, then, can the right decisions ever be reached by those who deny Him?

"For men swear by one greater than themselves; and an oath for confirmation is the end of all their controversy." (Hebrews 6:16)

◄§ Pray that the millions now practically unaware of God's existence may be given an increasing consciousness of Him.

226

WHY NOT THIS?

The president of one of America's great universities constantly refers in his talks to the *"search for truth."* Never once have we heard him refer, even in passing, to the immutable truths on which our nation is founded— truths so obvious that our Founding Fathers called them *"self-evident."*

Make your voice heard! The next time you hear or read of any person—especially one who has the great responsibility of leading others—ignoring the basic truth of our way of life, founded as it is on a profound belief in the existence of God, write him a friendly letter. In your own words urge him, for the good of the country, not to overlook or exclude those *"self-evident truths."*

Encourage him to do all the searching for truth he likes but not to lose sight of the all-important Truth that is always available for those who want it.

"You shall know the truth and the truth shall make you free." (John 8:32)

⚬§ Lord, help those who seek truth to find Thee, the Source of all Truth.

OVER AND OVER AGAIN

There is an ancient tradition about the last days of John the Evangelist. He lived to a great age and became so feeble he had to be carried to the meetings of the faithful. There, because of his weakness, he was unable to deliver a long discourse; so at each gathering he simply repeated the words: *"Little children, love one another."*

The disciples, weary of hearing the same words over and over, asked him why he never said anything else. And to them John gave this answer. He said, in effect, it is the commandment of the Lord: *"Do this alone and it is enough."*

If we adhered to these words the difficulty and complexity of our daily lives would disappear. In this clear advice we have the solution to all the problems that create hatred and strife among nations.

"Behold how good and how pleasant it is for brethren to dwell together in unity." (Psalm 132:1)

⊷§ Pray for the patience you need to be a peacemaker.

LIVING AND GIVING

Betsy Barton, who lost the use of both legs fourteen years ago in an automobile crash, said recently:

"It is my experience that suffering and pain are, unfortunately, the great character builders—not that suffering is good in itself, but because it often helps to shift our expectation of happiness from without to a search for it from within . . . Mystics, to achieve spiritual understanding, cleared the way by depriving themselves of things by their own will. But we are so suffocated with things and with distractions that the real pursuit of happiness is almost impossible . . . Happiness is primarily an inner state, an inner achievement. In other words, I would like to close by saying that the Kingdom of Heaven is within us."

Suffering may be the means whereby we achieve self-understanding. In the measure that we achieve self-understanding we are able to reach out with understanding to others. Happiness is not found in the pursuit of things or in the possession of things. It comes from *living* and *giving*, from suffering and participation in the sufferings of others.

"Through many tribulations we must enter into the kingdom of God." (Acts 14:21)

◄§ Pray that you will overcome suffering, not be overcome by it.

TELLING THE WORLD

Most of us have frequent occasion to be grateful to God for special blessings He has showered upon us. But how few show our gratitude by telling others of His goodness, urging them to take heart?

One small boy in Providence, Rhode Island, however, did "tell the world." He sent this message to the *Evening Bulletin*, which gave it a prominent display:

"Dear Sir: I prayed to God to make my mother get better and I want to thank God so when He reads the paper He can see it. From a little boy who loves God. May God thank you."

What mattered to the child, evidently, was that God should be publicly thanked. In this way he sent a heartening proof of God's care to thousands, who may not have been aware of it or who may have forgotten it.

"So let your light shine before men, that they may see your good works, and glorify your Father who is in heaven." (Matthew 5:16)

✍ Help me, Lord, to show my gratitude to Thee, by sharing with others the blessings Thou hast showered upon me.

WITH ALL OUR MIGHT

In *Your Life* magazine there is the story of two little girls who were in danger of being late for school. *"Let's stop and pray for God to get us there in time,"* one of them said.

"No," said the other, *"let's run with all our might, and pray while we're running."*

To pray effectively we must *mean* what we say. Obviously, the best way to show our intention is to make an effort in the right direction. If we are trying, God's help will not be absent. The supply of goodness is inexhaustible, always available, but we must show our own good will to put it into practice.

"Do you not know that the runners in the race course all run, but only one takes the prize? Run in such a way so that you may obtain it." (I Corinthians 9:24)

⋙ Pray that you may show your faith in action.

THE WHOLE OF LIFE

Christ avoided no one. He talked not only to his disciples and well-wishers, but to unbelievers, to those who distrusted him, and even to scoffers. He is seen at a marriage feast, in the market place, among the rich, and among the poor. He built always on the material that was at hand. He took people as they were.

Reading the New Testament one is inevitably impressed by one thing: a conviction that every human being, every human situation has its own character and its own value from Christ's point of view.

It is easy to talk with our friends, with those who understand us and think as we do. The real test comes when we must go among strangers and especially into situations which are hostile.

What a temptation there is to let the opportunity slip by! To say to ourselves, *"This isn't the right moment,"* or *"There's nobody here who wants to listen to me."* Every moment is the "right" one; every person deserves to be told the Truth.

"But they going forth preached everywhere: the Lord working withal, and confirming the word with signs that followed." (Luke 16:20)

৯৽ Pray that you will always be alert.

IT TAKES ON MEANING

A man in a chain gang, breaking stones under the broiling sun, has no ambition, no enthusiasm. And, for him, the never-ending monotony of his work is almost unendurable.

A sculptor, on the other hand, in chiseling a beautiful statue out of a block of marble, toils away with a high degree of fervor. Despite the fact that much of what he does is, of necessity, routine and mechanical, still the task of making cold stone glow with life is made interesting and enjoyable because he has a purpose. *Purpose makes the difference.*

However trivial the task, it can be made meaningful through the purpose we carry into our work. Those who take positions in the fields of influence—education, government, labor relations, and communications—with the one purpose of carrying Christ into the mainstream of life, can perform all the humdrum aspects of their work with a fine spirit, simply because of the goal which inspires them.

"You are the salt of the earth. But if the salt lose its savour, wherewith shall it be salted? It is good for nothing anymore but to be cast out, and to be trodden on by men." (Matthew 5:13)

❧ Lord, help me always to carry high purpose into my work.

"FOR THIS I WAS BORN"

No one can produce any magic formula to Christianize the world. Our Lord didn't intend it that way. All He asked us to do was to work out the means of bringing His teachings to every part of the globe and *"to every creature."* We don't have to manufacture our message, as do those who are in error. Christ has given us divine Truth. Our only business is *to distribute it.* He left that one big job in our hands and guaranteed an abundance of grace to aid us.

Down through history the extent of our success is a matter of record. Much has been accomplished . . . but far more still remains to be done. As bearers of Christ, it is still our privilege to say with Him:

" . . . For this was I born, and for this came I into the world, that I should give testimony to the truth. Every one that is of the truth heareth my voice." (John 18:37)

Pray that you may ever be ready to distribute truth.

TWO GRATITUDES

The late Edwin Arlington Robinson, distinguished American poet, once wrote of gratitude:

"Two kinds of gratitude: the sudden kind we feel for what we take, the larger kind we feel for what we give."

To most of us the first kind is the more familiar: that pleasure and warmth we feel when someone remembers us on a birthday or an anniversary, the delighted surprise at an unexpected gift.

But we would agree, surely, that the second gratitude, while more rare, is more wonderful. How fine we feel when we have the opportunity to brighten the life of another; we feel deeply *grateful* for the opportunity to show our good will and our sense of Christian charity.

"Remember the word of the Lord Jesus, how he said: It is a more blessed thing to give, rather than to receive." (Acts 20:35)

✍§ Grant me, O Lord, an understanding of what it means to give, of my possessions and of myself.

INSIST ON THIS

More than three hundred years ago, when rulers who believed in the divine right of kings were trying to subject the citizen to tyrannical despotism, one notable figure, Robert Bellarmine, rose to rebuke this harmful notion by outlining more clearly the Christian insistence upon the dignity and worth of each person. Here are his words:

". . . *political power, considered in general . . . comes from God alone . . . secondly . . . this power resides, as in its subject, immediately in the whole state . . . in the third place . . . by the same natural law, this power is delegated to one (individual) or several . . . in the fourth place . . . (in) individual forms of government . . . it depends on the consent of the people to decide whether kings, or consuls, or other magistrates are to be established in authority over them . . .*"

These principles, which are so like those of our Founding Fathers and which predated our own Declaration of Independence by almost two hundred years, should be doubly important to us today, faced as we are by the threat of totalitarianism.

"There is no power but from God." (Romans 13:1)

&⸞ Pray that our officers of government will have a sense of personal responsibility for the authority which they have from God.

"WATCH THE BEGINNINGS"

"Practice makes perfect" goes an old saying. But, like many a proverb, it contains only *part* of the truth. For example, the golfer who practices his shots badly will never become proficient. Or if a person drives an automobile badly, he will never become a good driver simply by continuing to drive that way.

It is always important to *"watch the beginnings."* A problem in arithmetic begun the wrong way will get progressively further away from the right answer. Again, if, in walking from New York to Washington, D.C., you start off in the direction of Boston, the more you walk the farther you will get from your goal.

A faulty habit is not acquired in a moment, but gradually. Therefore, it is most important for every Christopher to start soon in life to rid himself of bad traits before they become part of his character.

". . . he that contemneth small things, shall fall by little and little." (Ecclesiasticus 19:1)

◢ Give me to see the importance of trifles.

WANTED!

More to improve, fewer to disapprove.

More *"doers,"* fewer *"talkers."*

More to say *"it can be done,"* fewer to say *"it can't be done."*

More to inspire others with confidence, fewer to throw *"cold water"* on anyone taking even one step in the right direction.

More to get into the thick of things and "do something about it," fewer to sit on the side lines merely finding fault.

More to point out what's right, fewer to keep harping on what's wrong.

More to *"light a candle,"* fewer *"to curse the darkness."*

"Be not overcome by evil, but overcome evil by good." (Romans 12:21)

O Lord, keep me from the miserable habit of fault-finding.

DON'T WRITE ANYONE OFF

Christ, in His divine patience, never wrote anyone off. No matter how great the sinner, how deep-dyed the scoundrel, Our Lord meant His words for him as well as for the righteous.

Famous examples of this spring readily to mind. Mary Magdalene, the courtesan. Zaccheus, the wealthy publican. Paul, who "breathed out threatenings and slaughter" against the Christians. Even among the apostles themselves there were Peter, who denied Christ, and Judas, who betrayed Him. And Jesus, it should be emphasized, did not write off Judas. *Judas wrote off himself.*

Finally, one of the most moving episodes in the New Testament is that of the salvation of the thief on the cross. Even in His last agony Christ saw in a common criminal a germ of good that could grow into redeeming repentance.

"And Jesus said to him: Amen I say to thee, this day thou shalt be with me in paradise." (Luke 23:43)

&s Pray that you may be merciful, not censorious.

239

THERE'S STILL TIME

There are many who feel that it is too late for them to begin living for God and for their fellow men. They are too old, too much of life has gone by, they say, and add: *"I wish I'd done this twenty years ago. . . . But now it's too late."*

At the age of thirty-three--middle age, in his times--after living a life of sin and irreligion, St. Augustine became conscious of his terrible foolishness. But once aware of his previous years of wretchedness and wastefulness, he did not merely sit down and bewail the past. This would have been the easiest thing to do, by far. But St. Augustine's vision was too broad to be concentrated on mere self-deprecation.

Instead, St. Augustine took the love he had found in Christ, and reached out with it to all men. In his devotion to his new-found Master he more than undid the harm for which he had been responsible. He did not keep Christ's love to himself; he tried to give it to the whole world!

". . . men that have given their lives for the name of our Lord Jesus Christ." (Acts 15:26)

&3 Pray for the grace to persevere unto salvation.

HIS HEART WAS MOVED

The Apostle Paul is the classic example of the bearer of Christ. His driving purpose and his burning desire to share his love of Christ with all are instanced again and again in the story of his work.

Once, when he was waiting in Athens for his companions to join him, *"his spirit was roused within him at seeing the city given to idolatry."* (Acts 17:16)

Paul could have found excuses for idleness. He could have said he deserved a rest, or he could have said that he was only passing through Athens and in such a short time there was little he could do. But instead he went into the market place and began to talk with the people, exciting their curiosity until they invited him to speak.

His brief speech is a masterpiece of tactful yet uncompromising persuasion. *"Men of Athens,"* he begins, *"I perceive that in all things you are very religious . . ."* He refers to their idols and temples. Then he gets to the point by mentioning one Athenian altar inscribed to *"An Unknown God."* It is this God, Paul tells them, he has come to describe to them. The rest of the speech is a stirring exposition of Christ and His teachings.

". . . since He Himself gives to all life and breath and all things . . ." (Acts 17:25)

EVEN AT THE LAST HOUR

All the newspapers carried long stories about the death of a famous actor. Some of the articles summed up his brilliant career, others revived scandalous stories of his private life, and all of them told of his Christian burial and the church services attendant on it.

Indignant inquiries flooded those who had attended the actor at his death, demanding how a man who had lived such a flagrantly sinful life could be given a Christian burial.

The answer was simple. On his deathbed he had repented and received the last sacraments. As one writer said at the time: *"He made his peace. It does not devolve on any of us to review the case; that is God's province. Let us confine ourselves to prayer for this man and for all others facing God at the bar of eternal justice. Instead of demanding stern retribution for others, let us beg plenteous mercy for ourselves. We need it."*

". . . there shall be joy in heaven upon one sinner that doth penance, more than upon ninety-nine just that need not penance." (Luke 15:7)

ᕳ Lord, teach me not to judge others but to pray for God's mercy on them.

MOVING FAST

In one issue of a metropolitan daily recently the following headlines appeared:

"BOY, NINE, SLUGGED BY TWELVE-YEAR-OLD BANDIT" . . .
"WOMAN SOCIALITE RECOVERING AFTER SUICIDE LEAP" . . .
"THIRTEEN-YEAR-OLD GIRL DROWNS PLAYMATE" . . .

These are only signs of what is yet to come. Things will continue to get worse in direct proportion to the extent that parents and educators persist in neglecting to teach children self-control based on a sense of personal responsibility to God. Indications on all sides point to an ever-widening "moral paralysis" creeping over our nation. To argue that it is impossible to do anything about it on the grounds that conditions similar to this have always been part of our society is no argument at all. *Something can be done about it.*

Imperfect as people may be with the Commandments, they are no better off when they disregard them. A Christopher will strive to impress the world with the idea that we are accountable to God for every action we do on earth. God is merciful—but He is likewise *just!*

"For the Son of man shall come in the glory of His Father with Angels: and then will He render to every man according to his works." (Matthew 16:27)

⋧ Let Thy law be my meditation.

243

IT'S GOD'S IDEA

The English novelist H. G. Wells once called upon the American novelist Henry James. In the drawing room of James's house Wells noticed a large and peculiar stuffed bird.

"My dear James," he said, astonished, *"what is that?"*

"That," James replied, *"is a stork."*

"Humph," Wells snorted. *"It's not my idea of a stork."*

"Apparently, however," came the answer, *"it was God's idea of one."*

Frequently our idea of something may not be God's idea; subconsciously, we may even feel that *our* idea is better. But the Creator's plan is above our logic. When we accept it, we find ourselves quickly in tune with life, more able to act constructively, to create according to the will of God, instead of blundering along in our private confusion.

". . . For the ways of the Lord are right, and the just shall walk in them." (Osee 14:10)

ᴇᴣ Give us, O Lord, the wisdom to see thy ways, and the courage to walk therein.

THEY ARE ON THE JOB

In his book *The Man in the Street* the learned authority on American history, Professor Thomas A. Bailey of Stanford University, uttered this warning which should give us all food for thought:

"If the ordinary American citizen can only work himself up to a point where he is as deeply interested in the outer world—in the fate of his country, his civilization, and his planet—as he is in the doings of his next-door neighbor and his favorite comic-strip character, then we shall make greater progress towards a successful democratic foreign policy."

We are often tempted to let the rest of the world go by, caring only for ourselves, our families, and friends, ignoring issues and trends in the world around us.

Yet it is just such lack of interest of which the subversive elements make capital. *They* are interested; *they* read the papers; *they* listen to the radio; *they* never fail to vote; *they* write their congressmen. And *they* hope that the rest of us will stay in our own back yards. *Too often we please them far more than we suspect.*

"Lord, that our eyes may be opened." (Matthew 20:33)

❧ Pray that people in increasing numbers throughout our land will take a holy interest in all that concerns the welfare of mankind.

A LESSON TO LEARN

On a roadside in China a missioner saw a little eight-year-old girl being kicked and beaten by a crowd of bystanders because she was a leper. To the surprise of all, including the child, the missioner jumped to her rescue.

"Why do you bother about me?" the girl asked, when her tears had stopped. *"Why are you so kind?"*

"God made you and God made me," the missioner replied. *"He is your father and mine, so that makes us brother and sister. I'm going to see that you have everything God wants you to have. And there is only one thing He asks of you in return—to love Him and all men, good and bad, because they are your brothers and sisters too."*

The little leper girl learned that lesson in a few seconds and never forgot it. She died three years later, but her every waking minute before then was spent in caring for lepers worse off than she. At her funeral crowds came from all around the countryside to pay tribute to this child whom they affectionately called their *"little bit of heaven who has gone back to heaven."*

"Indeed, I tell you, as long as you did it to one of the least of these my brethren, you did it to me." (Matthew 25:40)

Pray for the billion and a half human beings over the world who have yet to hear that nineteen hundred years ago Christ was born, lived, and died for each of them.

LABOR SPEAKS

In 1943, in the midst of our war against the forces of totalitarianism, Philip Murray, president of the C.I.O., made this statement on Labor Day:

"We can speak of man's natural rights only if we recognize the truth of man's divine origin and his link with the eternal. If we deny this basic truth, we cut away the ground upon which rests the inviolability of human rights. Deny man's link with God and his transcendence over the merely temporal, and you forge for him the first link in the chain of servitude. You make him a mere cog . . . of the collectivity. You fall into the frightful error of those who believe, and assert with all the force of armed might that man is only a robot to further the interests of the greater whole, be it state or race."

More persons, aware of the danger into which any nation puts itself when the Origin of our rights is forgotten, are needed to repair the broken link between men and their Creator. And they are needed now!

❧ Pray that the common good will always be served both by labor and management.

THERE ALL THE TIME

One of the most authoritative dictionaries, published in 1944, carries this interesting definition of *uranium:*

"A rare, heavy, white metallic element . . . It is never found native, and has no important uses, although certain of its salts are used as pigments, especially in the manufacture of glass and porcelain."

"No important uses"—this is what was written a few years ago about what is today probably the most valuable metal in existence. Little did people realize then the tremendous importance of this single element. Nor did they realize the worldwide fear and awe in which, within a year or so, the very name *uranium* would be held.

It is wise never to judge by outward appearances. We ought not to judge even ourselves so. We may think we have *"no important uses."* Yet all the time there are within us untapped sources of excellence which, sparked by purpose and strengthened by the grace of God, will enable us to do tremendous things for Him.

◄§ Lord, let me never think I have no important uses; but help me to see what I can do for Thee.

OVEREMPHASIS ON SELF

Parents and teachers are so preoccupied with protecting the young that they overemphasize self-preservation, self-sanctification, self-development, and self-enjoyment. Without meaning any harm, they often give children the impression they have but one mission in life—to take care of themselves, and seldom stress their obligation to the common good of all—to "love thy neighbor as thyself."

Of course, as Thomas Aquinas said: *"A man must have a certain anxiety about the acquisition or preservation of external things."* Everyone *should have* a reasonable interest in nutritious food, proper clothing, good housing, and other necessities and comforts. But many so overemphasize their own interests that they seldom devote time and energy to provide the urgently needed personal leadership to win for the great masses of mankind—not conveniences or luxuries—the bare necessities of life which God intends as their minimum right.

Care of self is most important, but is only part of Christianity. By failing to pass on the fullness of Christ's message, many are fencing their children in, robbing them of the more abundant life God meant them to have.

&⸫ O Lord, broaden my vision to include, not to exclude, the souls of others in my own solicitude for an eternal reward of joy.

249

HARD TO BREAK

We've all had this happen to us: Try to break a piece of rope and find it too strong for us. Then the only thing to do is unravel the rope and break it strand by strand—a difficult and sometimes impossible procedure.

It's the same way with habits. Few of us indulge in really great deceits, but for many of us hardly a day goes by without our telling an "innocent" lie or committing some "harmless" act of dishonesty. But these insignificant sins build up a kind of tolerance in us, and soon we find our sense of right and wrong less sharp.

Good habits work the same way in reverse. If we get the habit of goodness, of performing small acts of kindness and generosity, we soon discover that goodness comes easy to us: in big things as well as small.

"A threefold cord is not easily broken." (Ecclesiastes 4:12)

Help me, O Lord, to snap the first thread of a bad habit before it is spun into an unbreakable cable.

THE LURE OF FLATTERY

To most of us *flattery* seems a trivial fault, innocent in its effect. But the Bible is specific in warning against it; and when we reflect, we realize it is indicative of a carelessness about truth that is grave indeed. A just estimate of others, sincere admiration, constructive criticism— these are attributes of truthful thinking.

1. *"As silver is tried in the fining-pot, and gold in the furnace: so a man is tried by the mouth of him that praiseth."* (Proverbs 27:21)

2. *"He that rebuketh a man, shall afterward find favor with him, more than he that by a flattering tongue, deceiveth him."* (Proverbs 28:23)

3. *"A prince that gladly beareth lying words, hath all his servants wicked."* (Proverbs 29:12)

4. *"It is better to be rebuked by a wise man, than to be deceived by the flattery of fools. . . ."* (Ecclesiastes 7:6)

5. *"For neither have we used, at any time, the speech of flattery, as you know; nor taken an occasion of covetousness, God is witness."* (I Thessalonians, 2:5)

❧ O Lord, teach me to bring assistance to others through sincere words of praise and constructive suggestions, and never to harm others through flattery.

MEN, NOT SYSTEMS

Many people in this world never really look at their fellow men. Usually such persons are not conscious at all of their fundamental lack of interest. Often they think of themselves as models of charity and kindness. Yet the fact remains that their unconcern for their neighbors and their problems is frequently the cause of immense suffering, sorrow, and hatred.

Some people regard Karl Marx as the champion of the poor and oppressed—a grossly false impression. As a close student of Marx's life and teachings has said:

"Marx's failure to look at the poor was only part of his general failure to look at men . . . he was not interested in men . . . he did not love men; but he was desperately in love with the System he had constructed for them."

Unfortunately, this often is as true of those who oppose Marxism as it was of Marx. Yet in the end the results are bound to be the same—slavery and death. To avoid this terrible fate, we must exercise a genuine love for every human creature.

❦ O Lord, enable me to see each person as an individual, and to love him for himself for love of You.

EXTERNAL APPEARANCES

A celebrated French artist who never bothered much with his appearance was out walking one morning when he heard a feminine voice behind him call: *"My good man, can you carry my bundle a little way for me?"* Turning, he saw a very beautiful woman; so, instead of explaining who he was, he said, *"Most willingly, madame,"* and took the bundle from her.

First into one shop then into another he followed her. Finally the woman came to her home and fumbled in her purse for some change. But when she offered it to him, the artist refused.

"Madame," he said, *"I am not a porter, despite the ungracious compliment you paid my appearance. I am an artist, and I shall be well repaid if I can make a copy of your beautiful face and send it to the next exhibition at the Academy."*

How easy it is to take external appearances as everything. And, to carry the point still further, how easy it is to forget the image of God in each of His creatures.

"Judge not according to the appearances, but judge just judgement." (John 7:24)

✑ Lord, teach me always to look upon Your image in others.

ABOVE ALL OTHERS

A Christopher will strive incessantly to bring to all men a realization of the existence of a personal God Who has spoken to the world and on Whom the world depends. This is the truth upon which mankind must base all hope for a better world. It is the truth the founders of our country reverently and repeatedly affirmed in the Declaration of Independence.

This truth is the one fundamental upon which all else depends. This is why every form of totalitarianism relentlessly opposes it and seeks to destroy man's faith in God.

This being so, then the one truth above all others which the Christopher should strive to carry into every phase of public and private life is the existence of a personal God Who, out of His superlative goodness, has revealed Himself.

"He disputed, therefore, in the synagogue, with the Jews, and with them that served God, and in the market place, every day with them that were there." (Acts 17:17)

❧ Pray that thousands will enter the market place to uphold belief in God, the First Truth.

ROOM FOR IMPROVEMENT

It is nearly fifty years since William James, one of America's pioneers in the field of psychology, pointed out that few persons ever make maximum use of their powers. Even the genius, he said, seldom uses more than 10 or 20 per cent of his capacity.

More recently an authority on labor problems pointed out that *"No man does the maximum amount of work of which he is capable, whether he be a common laborer, a college professor, or a president of a large corporation. Almost any man, from executive to floor mopper, could do in half a day what he now does in eight hours. And he would do it gladly if it did not involve for him ultimate loss rather than ultimate gain."*

It is challenging to the Christopher to be reminded of the ultimate gain which will be his if he works as hard to bring Christ's love into the market place as the subversives work to bring in hatred. This vision should give him the incentive to do twice as much as they do. The Communists have only a "World to Win"; we have the "World to Win" and "Heaven *too!*"

◆§ Lord, help me to remember I have a World to Win, that those far from Thee may have Heaven also.

DANGEROUS ATTITUDE

Not long ago we chanced upon a magazine photograph of two small children pressing their noses against the window of a toy store. The scene was from a current motion picture, and the caption underneath had the older child saying: *"Our new baby sister will never know the hard times we've known, will she?"*

"No, she won't," came the answer. *"But she'll never have the fun either."*

It is easy for all of us to sentimentalize over the hardships of others. Many writers today, through their attempts to glamorize poverty and misery, persuade a lot of people to do nothing for the common good. Not only are they forgetful of the wisdom of Thomas Aquinas who said: *"Involuntary poverty is one of the greatest of evils."* They likewise lead others into an attitude of inaction. And this policy puts the souls and bodies of millions into the hands of those bent on subversion.

The Christopher will ever strive to overcome this attitude in himself and in others.

⮞ Lord, help me to do what I can to lift the burdens of others so that they, with lighter heart, may go into the market place to bring there Your peace and love.

DON'T BE DISCOURAGED

We will seldom grow discouraged at the lack of interest in Christ we see in the world around us if we remember Christ's own words to those earlier Christ-bearers, the apostles. The night of His agony Jesus said:

"These things have I spoken to you that you may not be scandalized.

"They will put you out of the synagogues: yes, the hour cometh, that whosoever killeth you, will think that he doth a service to God.

"And these things will they do to you, because they have not known the Father, nor Me.

"But these things I have told you, that when the hour shall come, you may remember that I have told you of them.

"But I told you not these things from the beginning, because I was with you. And now I go to him that sent me, and none of you asketh me: Whither goest thou?

"But because I have spoken these things to you, sorrow hath filled your heart.

"But I tell you the truth: it is expedient to you that I go: for if I go not, the Paraclete will not come to you; but if I go, I will send him to you." (John 16: 1–7)

⇜ Help me to remember, O Lord, that those who serve Thee have been promised persecution as their lot.

UP THE STEEP SLOPES

Someone once asked Mallory, the famous climber who lost his life on Mount Everest, why he wanted to attempt to scale that mountain.

Mallory answered simply: *"Because it is there."*

The daring climber saw a challenge in the very existence of the uncharted peak, and something would not let him rest until he had attempted it.

Many of us would like to drift through life, taking it as it comes, following the easy path. But for others a challenge exists—the challenge to live creatively, to mold life into something worth-while. Like the climber, they see the difficulty and the hardship, but they see also the reward: a deep sense of accomplishment—the sense the Christian has when he carries Christ up the steep slopes and keeps in sight the end of the climb—the peak of eternity.

"Nor height, nor depth, nor any other creature shall be able to separate us from the love of God, which is in Christ Jesus our Lord." (Romans 8:39)

ᴥ§ Lord, teach me never to turn away from the challenge life offers to win souls back to You.

NEVER TOO LATE

Diogenes Laertius in his *Lives and Opinions of Eminent Philosophers* relates a story about the ancient thinker Lacydes.

It seems he began quite late in life to study geometry. Someone asked him about this. *"Is it then a time for you to be learning now?" "If it is not,"* the philosopher replied, *"when will it be?"*

The opportune moment is what we all wait for: the proper time to do this good deed, to begin that course of action. As a matter of fact, the fault does not lie in the moment but in our own lack of decision. It is never too early or too late to make up our minds to do the right thing, to set ourselves in a new and positive direction, headed toward Christ.

". . . forgetting the things that are behind, and stretching forth myself to those that are before, I press towards the mark, to the prize of the supernal vocation of God in Christ Jesus." (Philippians 3:13, 14)

Pray that the millions over the world who have forgotten may now remember that we begin our eternity here on earth.

NOT ALONE

Admiral Byrd, on one of his trips to Little America, spent months alone, apart from his party, living in a small cabin equipped with rough furnishings. He had no companion save the fierce Antarctic storms. Single-handed, he cleaned his cabin, checked his instruments, prepared his meals.

One is tempted, reading this, to think that Admiral Byrd was self-sufficient. Yet a little thought reveals how dependent he was upon others. He needed others to get him to Antarctica; to build his cabin; to keep in touch with him by radio. When he was dangerously ill, his men brought him medical aid. He was dependent, too, upon those who financed his project, on the farmers who raised his food, on the designers and manufacturers of his scientific instruments.

One of the weaknesses of our age is that of failing to recognize not only the social nature of man but, even more, man's dependence on God. However, each of us can do his part to restore that recognition, to bring to others the teaching of St. Paul: *"For none of us liveth to himself; and no man dieth to himself."* (Romans 14:7)

⋙ Pray that God will send into the market place at least a million Christ-bearers to restore to men their lost sense of brotherhood as children of one Father.

SO TYPICAL

When Victor Heiser was director of health in the Philippines one of his main tasks was to protect the water supply of Manila. One day he issued a notice that a new chlorination system for purifying the water would be installed on June 10. On June 11 complaints poured in to the Board of Health. *"The water is not fit to drink,"* was the recurrent theme, and the press promptly took up the cry.

"For a week and a half," says Dr. Heiser, *"we made no mention of a mishap"* which had delayed the introduction of the chlorine. *We then released the facts, stating that at last we were ready."*

Only then were the voices of protest silenced.

Typical, isn't it? Those who were in the Army know well the irritating habit of "griping" into which vast numbers of the men fell. Nothing that was done was ever good enough. Every change was resisted.

All of us are guilty, more or less, of this dangerous habit. It is a fault which lessens our own happiness and contributes to the unhappiness of others.

"Rejoice in the Lord always; again, I say, rejoice." (Philippians 4:4)

ᴥ§ Help me to remember, O Lord, that by my own cheerful acceptance of Thy will I may be able to bring others to make the world better.

ON THE TARGET

"With the time and energy we spend in making failure a certainty we might have certain success," said Dorothea Brande, an outstanding American writer, a decade or so ago. *"Suppose a man had an appointment a hundred miles north of his home,"* she went on, *"and that if he kept it he would be sure of having health, much happiness, fair prosperity, for the rest of his life. He has just time enough to get there, just enough gas in his car. He drives out, but decides that it would be more fun to go twenty-five miles south before starting out in earnest."*

The point she was making is quite obvious. It isn't enough merely to live: we must know our destination. It isn't enough, either, to have a vague idea of our destination, decide to go there sometime, but meanwhile dally along the way. We have just so much time allotted to us, just so much energy. It is up to us to move with a purpose, to choose the proper roads—the necessary means, and to keep right on moving.

"I therefore so run, not as at an uncertainty: I so fight, not as one beating the air." (I Corinthians 9:26)

ᥱᥤ Pray that you may use all your energies for good.

MORE THAN UNFAIR

Many perhaps never think of it in that way, but *punctuality* is a moral quality. *Unpunctuality* can be a serious lack of moral perfection. Once in a while, of course, anybody is apt to be late to work, to church, or for an appointment. Unpunctuality refers to the *habit* of being late.

To rid ourselves of this sometimes uncharitable and unjust habit we must get at its two main roots: first, the reluctance to submit to rules; second, the notion that we can cram many activities into a short period of time. Basically, unpunctuality is rooted in egotism, for the unpunctual person acts as though time should yield him obedience!

And since egotism is an exaggerated opinion of one's self, it can lead the way to another moral fault. It can hinder those who know Christ from bringing knowledge of Him to others who know Him not.

&§ Help us to remember, O Lord, that our time belongs to Thee and that, therefore, we have no excuse for wasting it.

HORIZONS

"*There is one task that only a world community can achieve—the never-ending and collective task of turning, first, into clear ideas all that human heads can think, and then into concrete things all that human hands can make.*"

These are not the words of a statesman of the twentieth century. They were written more than six hundred and fifty years ago by a man who has been loved and admired by millions for his world vision, his wisdom, his compassion. His name was Dante Alighieri, patriot and poet, soldier and statesman.

Anyone who grasps even a fraction of such broad vision and who strives to communicate it to others can be a channel of grace, an instrument of the peace and truth of Christ. For even Dante's world vision was but a reflection of the world vision of Our Lord. It is only because we are made in the image of God that we can reflect that vision of His at all. And each time we strive to bring some glimpse of it to others, we glorify Him in Whose image we are made.

⊸§ O Lord, in whose image we are made, grant that we may reflect in our daily lives Thy world vision.

80,000 HOURS

In a short time an editor of one of America's leading dailies will round out a career of forty years as a newspaperman. The high purpose and devotion that have always characterized his work and account in large measure for the great service he has rendered in influencing the lives of millions go back to a decision he made long ago, when graduating from college.

He felt he should take up an occupation where he could do more than earn a living. He felt he should be creative, should reflect into the lives of as many as possible the blessings God had bestowed upon him. Now as he nears the end of a career, during which he has averaged forty hours a week or two thousand hours a year at his job, he can look back on the impressive total of 80,000 hours spent in enriching the lives of others as well as his own.

It would be well to encourage anyone starting out on his life's work to select a career with the same purpose this editor had. And each of those who do will one day hear Christ saying to him: *"Well done, thou good and faithful servant; because thou hast been faithful over a few things, I will set thee over many; enter into the joy of thy master."* (Matthew 25:21)

⊷ Pray for the grace to live a life of high purpose.

NOT JUST ANOTHER JOB

A schoolteacher, an avowed Communist, recently boasted that for some forty years she had missed no opportunity to teach atheism in our public schools. She stated she is now an active member in every single Communist front listed by the Attorney General as subversive, and that to her teaching was *not* just another job. Her classes usually averaged fifty students, yet she bragged: *"I wasn't teaching just fifty students. I taught each and every boy and girl individually!"* And added: *"My only regret is that I don't have another forty years to teach."*

The driving force behind this woman's determination was her *sense of purpose*. From the misplaced industry of all the anti-God disciples over the earth we should take warning. There is nothing local-minded about them. Their vision is world-wide. They take a personal responsibility in changing the world itself, even if only from a classroom. On the other hand, for example, in the particular area where this teacher was located, it was recently discovered that while only 7 in 100 who practiced religion were going into the teaching field, *40 out of 100 were leaving it.*

Only as this trend is reversed and those with the knowledge of the Truth dedicate themselves to teaching our young will the foundations be laid for Christ's peace and justice here on earth, with a firmer hope for an eternity of happiness for them in heaven.

"The sons of this world are more clever in their own sphere than are the children of the light." (Luke 16:8)

⋧ Pray to be as generous in doing good as others are in doing evil.

EVEN UNTO DEATH

In Effingham, Illinois, on the night of April 5, 1949, there occurred one of the most tragic hospital fires in this country's history. Among the victims was a heroic twenty-two-year-old nurse, Fern Riley, who stayed at her post even though it eventually resulted in her death.

On the night of the fire she was on duty, caring for ten newborn babies in the second-floor nursery. When the alarm sounded, according to the newspaper accounts, someone heard her shout: *"My babies! I've got to stay with my babies!"*

Her body—what there was left of it—was still in the nursery when the fire at last burned itself out.

The selfless Christlike devotion to the weak and the helpless which Fern Riley showed, even unto death, should be an inspiration to those who sometimes may feel discouraged when the task of bearing Christ into the market place may run into obstacles and difficulties. Christ suffered and died for each of us. If need be, we should be willing to do as much for Him and for those of His "children" who may be helpless without our help.

"Greater love than this no man hath, that a man lay down his life for his friends." (John 15:13)

 Lord, give me the love that is stronger than death.

NO DISTINCTION

All of us should remember that with God there are no distinctions of class or race or nation, because He is the Father of all. As the Bible states:

1. *"The rich and poor have met one another: the Lord is the maker of them both."* (Proverbs 22:2)

2. *"The poor man and the creditor have met one another: the Lord is the enlightener of them both."* (Proverbs 29:13)

3. *"For God will not except any man's person, neither will he stand in awe of any man's greatness: for He made the little and the great, and he hath equally care of all."* (Wisdom, 6:8)

4. *"And Peter opening his mouth, said: In very deed I perceive that God is not a respecter of persons. But in every nation, he that feareth him, and worketh justice, is acceptable to him."* (Acts 10: 34–35)

5. *"For there is no distinction of the Jew and the Greek: for the same is Lord over all, rich unto all that call upon him."* (Romans 10:12)

6. *"Where there is neither Gentile nor Jew, circumcision nor uncircumcision, Barbarian nor Scythian, bond nor free. But Christ is all, and in all."* (Colossians 3:11)

•§ Cleanse my heart, O Lord, of all prejudice and narrowness that I may reach out with Thy love to all men.

THE CURE DIED

Several years ago an elderly doctor in New England discovered a remarkably effective cure for asthma which proved to be successful in eight out of every ten cases.

"Why, that's wonderful!" a friend congratulated him as soon as he heard of it. And then he suggested: *"But you ought to put it on the market so it can reach more people."*

The suggestion fell on deaf ears. The good doctor, preoccupied with his own small group of patients, neglected to take any measures to make his discovery available to millions. A short time later the doctor died and his cure, of course, died with him.

Limited vision and possessiveness on our part deprive countless others of blessings that God meant for them— and meant to get to them through us!

"Reject not the petition of the afflicted: and turn not away thy face from the needy." (Ecclesiasticus 4:4)

❧ Pray that you may never withhold whatever means you have for helping others.

OPPOSITION MEANS DEATH

Twelve years ago Leon Trotsky, the fiery revolution-
ist, second only to Lenin in the Revolution, penned this
surprising warning:

*"In a country where the sole employer is the State,
opposition means death by slow starvation. The old principle, who does not work shall not eat, has been replaced
by a new one: who does not obey shall not eat."*

It is sobering to think what life in our land would be
like if ever the forces of subversion were to accomplish
what they have set out to do. No one who dared oppose
those in power would know any security. Even a single
word of criticism of the authorities would result in
deprivation of the very necessities of life.

How can we meet this challenge save by taking it upon
ourselves (and encouraging others) to work as hard to
save our country as the evil are working to destroy
it? For this task a million Christ-bearers are needed: each
of us can—and must—play his part!

⊷§ O God, do Thou continually remind me that if I do
not play my part, someone else—intent on evil—may take
my place.

270

FLING AWAY AMBITION

Wolsey was Henry VIII's teacher in statecraft, the man who had made England a power to be reckoned with. But when there was no longer any need for him, the unscrupulous king did not hesitate to get rid of his former adviser. In Shakespeare's play, *Henry VIII*, the aging and worldly cardinal gives this advice to a young courtier:

"I charge thee, fling away ambition:
By that sin fell the angels; . . .
Love thyself last: cherish those hearts that hate thee; . . .
Had I but served my God with half the zeal
I served my king, He would not in mine age
Have left me naked to mine enemies . . ."

Self-reliance is a virtue that many justly admire, but to be really effective it must be rooted in faith in God. There is nothing wrong with ambition, if our desire is not a merely selfish one for worldly glory, but has always our eternal destiny in mind.

"Seek ye therefore first the kingdom of God, and his justice, and all these things shall be added unto you." (Matthew 6:33)

&§ Pray that your chief ambition will always be to help bring God to men and men to God.

DOUBLE–DEALING

A small item in the New York *Times* told a disturbing story. *"Publicity Concern Plays Both Sides in Labor Rows"* was the headline; then the story went on to explain how a public-relations organization in recent strikes had been engaged by opposing sides and had, on different days, given out publicity releases, some of which took violent issue with management, others which were equally violent against the unions.

Surely we all know people of whom this reminds us: those whose convictions change from one day to the next, yet they are always argumentative no matter what side they currently happen to be defending. Being changeable is not necessarily the sign of an "open mind"; those whose convictions continually vary are likely not to have any convictions at all. People whose lives have a basis of divine truth and belief may change their minds about the lesser things, but they remain firm at heart and quietly command the respect of others of weaker principles.

"But the sure foundation of God standeth firm . . ."
(II Timothy 2:19)

⊸§ Pray that your faith may be steadfast.

WORSE THAN THE FIRST

In 1940 Max Eastman, Lenin's one-time friend, found himself forced to admit that

"*. . . instead of being better, Stalinism is worse than Fascism, more ruthless, barbarous, unjust, immoral, anti-democratic, unredeemed by any hope or scruple.*"

After six long, cruel years, World War II came to an end in August 1945. Everyone was hoping that the threat to freedom had at last been crushed. Soon, however, all of us came to see clearly that a new and far more terrible threat faced our country—faced each and every one of us.

The solution: Our Lord put it this way:

"*When an unclean spirit is gone out of a man he walketh through dry places seeking rest, and findeth none. Then he saith: I will return into my house from whence I came out. And coming he findeth it empty, swept, and garnished. Then he goeth, and taketh with him seven other spirits more wicked than himself, and they enter in and dwell there: and the last state of that man is made worse than the first. . . .* (Matthew 12:43–45)

If we would not have the world filled with the error that destroys, we must fill it with the truth which is life.

Pray that God will supply the world with enough Christ-bearers who will seek not merely to oppose Communism but to erect a truly Christian society in every land.

WATCH THE NOTICES

A man in one of our large cities received from the Bureau of Internal Revenue a "Second Notice" that his tax payment was overdue. The notice carried with it dire threats as to what would be done if the payment was not forthcoming immediately. Hurrying to the Collector's office, the man paid up and said: *"I'd have paid this before but I didn't get your first notice."*

"Oh," replied the clerk, *"we've run out of first notices, and besides, we find the second notices are a lot more effective."*

When we think back, we can recall many "first notices" that God has given us which we have ignored; perhaps an opportunity missed or a warning not heeded brought trouble because we were just too complacent or selfish.

It's human nature to wait until the lightning has hit the roof before we take out insurance. If we're lucky enough to have a third warning, the premium has gone up so far the price that must be paid means compromise and sacrifice. The accounting will be all the more difficult when we are called.

"For what doth it profit a man, if he gain the whole world, and suffer the loss of his own soul? Or what shall a man give in exchange for his soul?" (Matthew 16:26)

"Today you shall hear his voice, harden not your hearts." (Psalm 94:8)

◆§ Lord make me alert to Thy inspiration.

IT'S YOUR COUNTRY

The electorate means all those who are eligible to vote. To be a part of it is to be the inheritor of a great tradition, a precious privilege purchased by long struggle and suffering. But just as many nowadays neglect other rights so do many neglect their right to vote. *They abuse the privilege by neglecting it.* In the presidential election of 1900, for example, 75 per cent of the electorate voted. In 1944, however, only 55 per cent voted. In the 1946 congressional election only 30 per cent made use of their ballot.

This means if only 30 per cent of the electorate votes, then 15 per cent of the eligible voters can select the spokesmen who are to *govern* the nation. Thus 85 per cent of the people are taking orders from 15 per cent. And this 15 per cent could hardly be blamed if they should suddenly conclude that a democracy in which three quarters of the voters don't care about their rights is ripe for dictatorship.

It is your responsibility—and your privilege—as a voter to be able to say what you want. As a Christopher, be sure that you support the spiritual foundation on which our government is based. And be sure you urge others to follow your example.

"There is no authority that is not from God." (Romans 13:1)

⋖ Pray that all the citizens of our land eligible to vote may take this privilege as their duty.

REACHING EVERYBODY

A few summers ago I was in a group which went from Paris to the little town of Lisieux. Much of it was destroyed by the war, but not the convent where a little French girl had entered at fifteen and died at twenty-four: Thérèse of Lisieux, the Little Flower of Jesus. She, probably more than anyone else who has lived in our day, has reached millions simply by loving everybody the world over. In some mystic way they came to know of her, to feel sure that she cared for each of them individually.

Her whole secret is expressed in her own words inscribed above her tomb: *"I would like to spend my heaven doing good on earth."*

She understood the important difference between merely *"being"* good and *"doing"* good; between being just a "hearer" and not a "doer." And because she wanted to reach others with her love, the Lord blessed her. Once you start *"doing"* good, you deepen, strengthen, and increase your *"being"* good. You, too, will start to reach out in love to all men as far as you can. It may well be, then, that God will bless you as He has blessed Thérèse.

"But be ye doers of the word, and not hearers only. . . ." (James 1:22)

⋙ Lord, help me to spend my whole life on earth bringing You to as many as I can.

STILL FRESH

Like countless others, Albert Cox of Washington, D.C., found great inspiration in this 700-year-old prayer of St. Francis of Assisi:

"Lord, make me an instrument of Thy Peace!
Where there is hatred . . . let me sow love
Where there is injury . . . pardon
Where there is doubt . . . faith
Where there is despair . . . hope
Where there is sadness . . . joy!
O Divine Master, grant that I may not so much seek
To be consoled . . . as to console
To be understood . . . as to understand
To be loved . . . as to love, for
It is in giving . . . that we receive
It is in pardoning . . . that we are pardoned
It is in dying . . . that we are born to eternal life."

Mr. Cox had a longing to share with others his own source of inspiration. In true Christopher fashion he decided to do something about it. He sent it to *This Week* magazine. Even if they turned it down, at least he was trying, and God blesses those who try.

Much to his delight, not only did *This Week* print the prayer in its seven million copies, but the *Reader's Digest*, in its fifteen million copies, reprinted it with tribute to Mr. Cox. Bickford's Cafeterias in New York City distributed it to thousands of its customers. *This Week* said that of all the selections they had published, none brought as great a response as this simple prayer.

≈§ Lord, help me to share with others the joys Thou hast given me.

277

THINK BEFORE YOU SPEAK

A young man lying on a hospital stretcher just before his operation turned to a sympathetic lady who stood near by and said: *"I'm so nervous. This is my first operation."*

"So am I," said the lady; *"my husband is the doctor and it is his first operation too."*

One important expression of true love for others, which this doctor's wife seems to have forgotten, is *tactfulness:* saying or doing what is encouraging, not discouraging; being honest without being brutal; showing a Christlike consideration for the feelings of others (no matter how mistaken they may be); and avoiding abruptness and sarcasm.

Tactfulness is a habit which can be developed anywhere—in the home, the factory, the office, the school.

"Even so the tongue is indeed a little member and boasteth great things. Behold how small a fire kindleth a great wood." (James 3:5)

⋖§ Lord, help me always to show regard for the feelings of others.

A RICH CARGO

On the docks of Gloucester, Massachusetts, a man from the city and a grizzled fisherman were watching two vessels come home through the fog.

The first ship was high and graceful, moving easily through the sea. The second, heavy-laden and listing, groaned through the mist.

To the stranger the first ship seemed the more impressive, but to the practiced eye of the fisherman, the slow, heavy movement of the second ship meant that she contained a rich cargo, that she had dared the deep waters where the quantities of fish wait for the enterprising crew.

To many of us the shallow water may seem more attractive, the easier job more alluring, but when we *"launch out into the deep"* we discover that the real reward is there, in the fuller labor of spreading Christ's truth and love.

"Launch out into the deep and lower your nets for a catch." (Luke 5:4)

&§ O God, teach me to be a fisher of men.

WRONG BOTH WAYS

There is an old French expression, *"The absent are always wrong."*

This proverb should have a special significance for all followers of Christ. They, above all others, should be, like Christ, interested in everybody's welfare, *not just their own.* Consequently, they should be found in greater numbers than all others in those vital fields which involve the well-being of the vast majority of mankind—education, government, labor management, and writing.

It is a bad sign when the followers of Christ are absent from these fields in normal times. But it is *far worse* for them to remain aloof in dangerous times like the present, when the godless are swarming into them as apostles of evil.

Yes, the *"absent are always wrong."*

"I pray not that thou shouldst take them out of the world, but that thou shouldst keep them from evil." (John 17:15)

⋘ Pray that each of us will become ever more aware that our *"doing nothing"* may cause more disaster than what the enemies of Christ are actually doing.

"THAT'S WHAT I WAS TAUGHT"

Year after year the outlook of 30,000,000 young Americans is determined in large measure by their teachers. The students are looking for the truth and put implicit faith in their instructors to impart it to them. Whatever is in the teachers' heads—good or bad—passes into theirs. Drinking in as gospel truth almost every pronouncement the teachers make, yet seldom knowing whether what they give them is the truth or not, they accept their teachers' word as the final authority. *"That's what I was taught"* is so often the only basis for the whole course of their lives.

What a frightening responsibility faces the rank and file of *good Americans*. If the teachers of America do not come from their midst, then we are handing over the future of our country to the very ones whose ultimate objective is to destroy it, for these latter are the ones who are going into the teaching profession in increasing numbers.

"Teach me goodness, discipline, and knowledge." (Psalm 118:66)

✑ Pray that God may send into the field of education those whose objective is to restore Christ to the market place.

SELF–RELIANT

The town of Teaneck, New Jersey, in a recent drive for cancer research, was astonished to learn that the most indefatigable worker was a widow who had been blind for thirteen years.

This woman, however, saw nothing unusual in what she had done. *"After all,"* she told a reporter who came to interview her, *"I was taught to be self-reliant and I can distinguish between light and shadow, so I am not altogether helpless. . . . There is much that I can do . . . and thank God I never was one to be sad. My blindness came over me gradually and I consider myself lucky to have had so many years of sight."*

By praying for God's guidance, we can learn, as this remarkable woman did, to "count our blessings" and to see the good side of our situation in life, whatever it may be.

"And let the peace of Christ rejoice in your hearts, wherein also you are called in one body: and be ye thankful." (Colossians 3:15)

⋙ Pray that *you* may learn to "count *your* blessings."

QUICK THINKING

A quick-witted girl made headlines a couple of years ago when she stopped a locomotive from crashing into a Flying Fortress as the plane made a forced landing on railroad tracks near Charlotte, North Carolina. The passengers escaped without serious injury, but were aghast when they saw a locomotive rushing toward the crippled plane.

Most of the spectators were frozen into inaction. One man did run out and wave his arms ineffectually, but the girl seized a broom from the hands of a curious housewife, thrust it into a bonfire, and gave it to a section hand to signal the onrushing engine. There wasn't much more than a foot between the train and the plane, but the girl had done her job.

Sometimes sudden and unusual situations seem bigger than we. We are inclined to shrug and say, *"What can I do by myself?"* Actually we never know our own capacity until we try. With confidence and courage we can surprise even ourselves.

> *"We never know how high we are*
> *Till we are called to rise. . . ."* Emily Dickinson

⋙ Lord, give me the grace ever to be alert to the countless opportunities to do Thy will.

THE SOUND APPROACH

In 1639 the citizens of Connecticut drew up what has been called "the first written constitution which established a government of free men by themselves." And, like the other founders of our nation, they based government upon God. The document in its original form reads, in part:

"Forasmuch as it hath pleased Allmighty God . . . that we . . . are . . . dwelling in and uppon the River of Conectecotte and the Lands thereunto adioyneing; And well knowing where a people are gathered togather the word of God requires that to mayntayne the peace and union of such a people there should be an orderly and decent Government established according to God . . . doe therefore assotiate . . . as one Publike State or Commonwealth; . . ."

Fired with this same spirit, thousands are needed *today* to participate in the affairs of government. And the urgency now is greater than it was back in the early days of our country. It is up to us!

"Give ear, you that rule the people . . . For power is given to you by the Lord . . ." (Wisdom 6:34)

◆§ Pray that more will go into government with the purpose of preserving our nation *"established according to God."*

TO THE MANY

Throughout the gospel story, as a kind of undercurrent, there is an urgency, emphasized by Christ, of reaching the "many," not merely a "select few." Repeatedly we read of His preaching to "multitudes," of the crowds that flocked to Him everywhere He went.

Christophers should be especially impressed by His going to those who disagreed with Him, for as He said: *"And other sheep I have, that are not of this fold: them also must I bring, and they shall hear my voice!"* (John 10:16)

Fired by this divine purpose, His disciples followed in His footsteps, preaching to crowds and spreading the word: *"And the multitude of believers had but one heart and one soul . . ."* (Acts 4:32)

There are still "multitudes" in the world who have not heard His word. It is the job of all who believe in Him to do more than just believe, to share their belief with those who do not have it.

⮑ Pray that Christ's truth may soon be shared by all men of all nations.

READY FOR THE WORST

A doctor tells this story of an eight-year-old boy whose sister was dying of a disease from which the boy himself had recovered some time before. Realizing that only a transfusion of her brother's blood would save the little girl, the doctor asked the boy: *"Would you like to give your blood for your sister?"*

The child hesitated for a moment, his eyes wide with fear. Then, finally, he said: *"Sure, Doctor, I'll do it."*

Only later, after the transfusion was completed, did the boy ask hesitantly, *"Say, Doctor, when do I die?"* Then the doctor understood the momentary hesitation and fear. It had taken the boy that long to decide to sacrifice his life for his sister.

Heroic bravery isn't limited only to grownups or to soldiers or firemen. It takes real courage to face sacrifice, to be willing to give ourselves up for others.

". . . strait is the way that leadeth to life." (Matthew 7:14)

⇌§ Pray daily to see opportunities for sacrifice and for the strength of soul to meet them.

LAUNCH OUT INTO THE DEEP

Many passages in the gospels have special meaning for Christophers. One in particular tells how Simon Peter was suddenly turned from a state of fearful caution in which he was accomplishing little to one of daring faith that brought about astonishing results.

"Now when he had ceased to speak, he said to Simon: Launch out into the deep, and let down your nets for a draught.

"And Simon answering said to him: Master, we have laboured all the night, and have taken nothing; but at thy word I will let down the net.

"And when they had done this, they enclosed a very great multitude of fishes, and their net broke.

"And they beckoned to their partners that were in the other ship, that they should come and help them.

"And they came, and filled both the ships, so that they were almost sinking.

"Which when Simon Peter saw, he fell down at Jesus' knees, saying: Depart from me, for I am a sinful man, O Lord.

"For he was wholly astonished, and all that were with him, at the draught of the fishes which they had taken.

"And so were also James and John the sons of Zebedee, who were Simon's partners. And Jesus saith to Simon, Fear not: from henceforth thou shalt catch men.

"And having brought their ships to land, leaving all things, they followed him. (Luke 5:4–11)

≈§ Lord, teach me to accept Thy word readily, as Peter did.

A QUICK CHANGE

There are several significant lessons for every Christopher in the conversation between Christ and Peter quoted yesterday for your reflection and prayer.

1. Peter was skeptical at first. Discouraged, he said: *"Master, we have labored all the night, and have taken nothing."* But he did not add that he and his companions had been in the safe, shallow waters where the fish are fewer.

2. Then, suddenly, Peter seemed to catch himself, to realize Christ was bidding him to be daring. At once he turned from cynical protest to brave faith: *". . . but at thy word I will let down the net."*

3. Out into the deep, dangerous waters, where storms are alarmingly sudden and frequent, they launched. Then they let down their nets. The result? *". . . And they came, and filled both the ships so that they were almost sinking."*

(continued tomorrow)

◄§ Lord, give me confidence always in Thy power and support.

A QUICK CHANGE (continued)

The story of the draught of fishes could have ended simply with the recording of the catch. But there was more to it than that. The real meaning of the incident, its demonstration of the power of faith, comes in the following verses:

4. Peter, *"wholly astonished"* at the big haul which resulted from a shift, at Christ's insistence, from the shallow to the deep waters, could not restrain himself. He *"fell down at Jesus' knees, saying: Depart from me, for I am a sinful man, O Lord."*

5. Christ's response to this was quick and inspiring. To this poor fisherman, who was to become the head of His Church, He then and there gave the most subime commission with which any man could be entrusted: *"Fear not, from henceforth thou shalt catch men."*

6. In the few closing words of the narrative much is summed up: *"And having brought the ships to land, leaving all things, they followed him."*

❧ Lord, give me the courage of humble faith.

"SHOULD I SWEAR FALSELY . . ."

A state supreme court justice spoke recently about the oath witnesses take in court. Few people nowadays take it seriously, he complained. Then he went on to show us an earlier oath, used by American courts in the last century. It goes:

"I do solemnly appeal to God, as a witness of the truth and the avenger of falsehood, and shall answer for the same at the great day of judgment, when the secrets of all hearts shall be known, that the evidence which I shall give in the case now on trial shall be the truth, the whole truth, and nothing but the truth, so help me God, upon penalty of the eternal damnation of my soul should I swear falsely."

If more witnesses today thought of their duties in the solemn light of this oath, surely justice would function more efficiently here.

"And the fruit of justice is sown in peace. . . ." (James 3:18)

☙ O Lord, Whose judgments are always just, teach me to seek justice in all my acts.

A DAY OF RECKONING

During the recent war a Japanese Foreign Office representative in China confided to an American correspondent that *"the Chinese could never be permanently subdued while Christians were able to preach their doctrine of faith and hope."*

"We have tried brutality and we have tried friendly propaganda," the Japanese representative went on to complain. *"But we get nowhere because too many Chinese have been told there inevitably will be a day of reckoning for us, when good will finally triumph over evil. This is the nonsense we must silence if we hope to remain here."*

Belief in the eventual victory of the forces of light over the hordes of darkness instills a determination that should enable us to fight on through the most discouraging difficulties. Since subversives the world over strive incessantly to destroy Christianity because they see it teaches each individual the faith, hope, and charity which are the chief obstacles to the promotion of their evil doctrine, it is all the more reason why we should pray and work without ceasing to bring Christ into the market place. If we do, the day of "peace on earth" may be not long delayed.

❧ Pray for the millions who are without hope.

FOLLOWING THEIR PATH

Some years ago a group of five boys in Rome were exploring the ancient catacombs beneath the city. Their lantern burned up all its fuel, and for two days and two nights the boys tried in vain to find a way out.

On the third day, tired, hungry, and frightened, they began groping on their hands and knees. Suddenly they discovered smooth places worn in the rock floor of the ancient passage. It was the path followed by the early Christians, who had come there for their devotions centuries before. Feeling out this path, the boys crawled to safety and the light of day.

When we feel lost and afraid sometimes, and the darkness of daily life seems to be closing around us, we might think of those early Christians: their sacrifices, trials, and martyrdoms. That should bring light into our darkness and give us the inspiration to set newly ablaze our own faith.

". . . Did we not walk in the same spirit? did we not in the same steps?" (II Corinthians 12:18)

➳ Pray that our Lord will give us the strength to walk in the paths of the martyrs.

ONLY ONE CURE

The great weakness of American education, according to Dr. Howard B. Jefferson, president of Clark University and a former Baptist minister, is its failure to give some kind of faith to college students. In a recent address he said:

"When religion was dethroned from its place of supreme importance, it could no longer serve as the unifying basis for all human activities and all branches of knowledge.

"So each form of activity worked on its own methods and defined its own ends, without reference to other activities and without reference to ultimate purpose, and without reference to life as a whole."

What this educator said about American colleges applies to our daily life in general. All of us tend to become self-centered, to lose our perspective on life as a whole. In the final analysis only faith can give us direction and purpose, whether in teaching or learning or living.

"Take heed therefore that the light which is in thee be not darkness." (Luke 11:35)

◄§ Lord, let me see all earthly learning as a reflection of Thy glory.

293

IN REVERSE

A successful businessman who could have brought much happiness into others' lives as well as his own made a revealing reply one day to a friend who had been trying to help him show more concern for the common good and less for his own selfish interests.

"*I can't figure out what you mean,*" the businessman said. "*I am interested in others. I do everything I can to make everybody like me.*"

Little did he realize how completely he had missed the point. He was frankly admitting that his only aim was to make everybody "*like him.*" He was unaware that it was his Christian duty first to "*like others.*"

The devil finds it easy to tempt us to the effort of *attracting* attention rather than *giving* attention to others. Pray that you will never succumb to this ruse of taking yourself too seriously and others not seriously enough. In proportion as you love others "*as you love yourself,*" so will you be happy here and hereafter.

"*If I . . . have not charity, I am become as sounding brass or a tinkling cymbal.*" (I Corinthians 13:1)

Lord, teach me to love others, whether or not they love me.

RICHES IN HIS HAND

There is an old legend about Aaron, a fisherman, who lived on the banks of a river. Walking home with his eyes half-closed one evening after a hard day's toil, he was dreaming of what he would do when he became rich. Suddenly his foot struck against a leather pouch filled with what seemed to him small stones. Absentmindedly he picked up the pouch and began throwing the pebbles into the water.

"When I am rich," he said to himself, *"I'll have a large house."* And he threw a stone. He threw another and thought, *"I'll have servants and wine and rich food."*

This went on until only one stone was left. As Aaron held it in his hand, a ray of light caught it and made it sparkle. He realized then that it was a valuable gem, that he had been throwing away the real riches in his hand while he dreamed idly of unreal riches in the future. All of us hold in our hands the power to enrich our lives and, above all, our lives in eternity.

". . . he that is hungry dreameth, and eateth, but when he is awake, his soul is empty." (Isaias 29:8)

Lord, make me alert to the opportunities at hand to help others and do Thy will.

DIVIDING AND SUBDIVIDING

The lovely flowering shrub, the fuchsia, was introduced into England by an old nurseryman who heard from a friend one day that an extraordinary flower of rich crimson and deep purple had been brought from the West Indies to a lady he knew. This so aroused the nurseryman's curiosity that he went to the owner of the plant and, after much persuasion, bought it from her. Immediately he stripped it of flowers and buds, divided it into cuttings which he forced in hotbeds, redivided, subdivided, and cultivated with care, skill, and perseverance.

At the next flowering season his labors were well rewarded by the genuine pleasure shown by visitors to his exhibition of three hundred healthy plants, which were proudly displayed in his show window.

When we have something we value, especially the blessing of faith, we may overlook what joy it would give others to possess it. Yet we should try to cultivate and develop it and strive to see that this joy may be shared by many.

"But he that received the seed upon good ground, is he that heareth the word and understandeth, and beareth fruit, and yieldeth the one an hundredfold, and another sixty, and another thirty." (Matthew 13:23)

෴ Pray that you may know the joy that comes from sharing with others.

SOMETHING MISSING

In the window of a United States Army Recruiting Station in a large southwestern city is this list of reasons why young men should join the service:

GOOD PAY	RETIREMENT
MEDICAL CARE	VACATIONS
EDUCATION	TRAINING ADVANCEMENT
TRAVEL	

To stress these attractions further, the poster bore the words: *"Check these United States Army Benefits—Plan for Your Future Now."*

It is easy enough to understand why these inducements were pointed out. There is no reason why the wealthiest nation in the world should not have the best-paid, best-fed, best-cared-for army.

But in the whole display there wasn't a single reference to the higher motives which can be stirred up in any young American, but which are more and more being sidetracked: devotion to a cause; service to country and to one's fellow citizens; patriotism.

You can do much, by prayer and work, to help change this trend toward playing up what one *takes out* and playing down what each should *put in*.

"For what things a man shall sow, those also shall he reap. . . ." (Galatians 6:8)

⊷ Lord, give me a desire to enrich the world in return for the privilege of living in it.

ARE YOU LISTENING?

His companions were making fun of the ragged barefoot boy. "*You're a Christian,*" they taunted him. "*If God really loves you, why doesn't He take better care of you? Why doesn't He tell someone to send you a pair of shoes?*"

The boy seemed puzzled for a moment. Then, with tears in his eyes, he replied, "*I think He does tell people. But they're not listening.*"

Those who strive to grow closer to Our Lord in prayer should find their minds and hearts growing larger each day. Their vision will take in more and more of life; their hearts will embrace more and more of their fellows.

Of course there is always the danger—one sees its effects too often—that those who strive to develop their inner lives will do so at the expense of consideration for their fellow men. To them the words of the Apostle John are most applicable:

"*And this commandment we have from God, that he, who loveth God, love also his brother.*" (I John 4:21)

Pray that you will develop that love of Christ, and in turn, pass it on to others.

THE FIRST VOTE

Some time ago Paul Antonio, a tinsmith, was hired to build and install the black steel ballot box now used by members of the United Nations Security Council at Lake Success when they cast their votes on world issues.

When the box was opened just before the first Security Council session, there was found at the bottom a brief message written in a clear handwriting on a cheap piece of notepaper. The message read:

May I, who have had the privilege of constructing this ballot box, cast the first vote? May God be with every member of the United Nations Organization, and through your noble efforts bring lasting peace to us all—all over the world."

(Signed) Paul Antonio, mechanic

By this one simple act did Antonio (a plain workman, like Joseph, the foster father of Jesus) give the Council members a reminder of the importance of the supernatural. At the same time (because the incident was widely publicized for its human-interest angle) he got the same lesson over to millions in our land and throughout the world.

"My peace I give unto you, not as the world giveth do I give unto you." (John 14:27)

❧ Pray that you may be alert to every opportunity to bring to others the true message of peace.

THE WAY TO DO IT

With love of God for his supreme motive, the Christopher proves his love for his fellow men by performing works of mercy, spiritual and corporal. He does this by:

1. Feeding the hungry
2. Giving drink to the thirsty
3. Clothing the naked
4. Visiting the imprisoned
5. Sheltering the homeless
6. Visiting the sick
7. Burying the dead

Our Lord explicitly taught that one can please God by performing these corporal works of mercy. He made it plain that anyone who deliberately refused to perform these works will enjoy no happiness hereafter.

One may, as the Catechism tells us, perform these works in many ways, *"not only by actually providing the necessities of life but also by working to correct economic abuses which cause unnecessary unemployment and poverty . . . by providing the necessary medical care . . . hospitals for the poor and home-nursing organizations. . . ."*

No matter how one performs these works, the important thing is that the motive be *love of God.*

"And the second is like it. Thou shalt love Thy neighbor as thyself." (Matthew 22:39)

⋐ Pray that you may have sympathy for others and may express it effectively.

THE WAY TO DO IT (*continued*)

More worthy even than the corporal works of mercy are those spiritual works which refer directly to the eternal welfare of men:

1. To admonish the sinner
2. To instruct the ignorant
3. To counsel the doubtful
4. To comfort the sorrowful
5. To bear wrongs patiently
6. To forgive all injuries
7. To pray for the living and the dead

By their very nature the spiritual works of mercy excel the corporal works, since they concern, directly, man's soul and his eternal welfare. They help to heal the soul and keep it from spiritual disease. They are the perfect fulfillment of Christ's command to love our neighbor.

These tasks should ever be uppermost in the minds of those who would bear Christ to all mankind.

"They that instruct many to justice shall shine as stars for all eternity." (Daniel 12:3)

⊷ Pray for insight into the spiritual needs of others.

HERE ARE THE FACTS

A recent report by the Statistical Office of the United Nations gave the population of the earth as 2,320,000,000 as of 1947—"the latest year for which figures for the entire world are available." According to the 1949 *World Almanac* approximately 600,000,000 persons profess some belief in Christianity or are "on the books" of some Christian religion. In addition, there are approximately 15,000,000 persons in the world of the Jewish faith.

The remainder—some 1,700,000,000 souls—have yet to hear of God at all. This is a startling fact, especially since nineteen centuries have rolled by since Christ explicitly commanded: *"Go ye into the whole world, preach the gospel to every creature."* (Mark 16:15)

But the figures speak for themselves. Furthermore, it is a recognized fact that those in pagan lands are increasing at the rate of 10,000,000 a year, probably ten times faster than we are reaching them. In short, the Christianization of the world at present is getting farther and farther away from us. Why? Is it because we are preoccupied with what is being done, and overlook what is *not* being done?

You can answer that challenge in your own way.

⋙ O God, Who desirest that all men should be saved and come to the knowledge of Thy truth, send, we beseech Thee, laborers into Thy harvest.

302

FOLLOW THE SIGNS

When Britain was in danger of invasion early in the war, the people were told to destroy all signposts and direction indicators in the countryside in order to confuse enemy paratroopers, should they land. In 1944, as soon as the danger had passed, the signs were immediately restored, since they were really vital to the successful life of the country.

Just as we cannot travel about the country without signs, so we cannot make our journey through life without some laws to tell us the right direction to follow. A disordered life is like a journey that has no destination. Fortunately, God has given us clear signs: the Natural Law, the Commandments, and above all the teachings of Christ. These markers make the route clear to all of us; we have only to follow them.

"I am the way, and the truth, and the life. No man cometh to the Father, but by me." (John 14:6)

⋙ Pray that you keep the sight of the Cross always in your mind's eye, so that you can be sure you are headed in the right direction—to your eternal salvation.

A DOUBLE WARNING

One of the most urgent warnings in Holy Scripture—
that of St. Paul to the Ephesians—is the necessity of
"putting on the armor of God" in order to *"stand against
the deceits of the devil."*

*"Finally, brethren, be strengthened in the Lord, and
in the might of his power.*

*"Put you on the armour of God, that you may be able
to stand against the deceits of the devil.*

*"For our wrestling is not against flesh and blood; but
against principalities and powers, against the rulers of the
world of this darkness, against the spirits of wickedness
in the high places.*

*"Therefore take unto you the armour of God, that you
may be able to resist in the evil day, and to stand in all
things perfect.*

*"Stand therefore, having your loins girt about with
truth, and having on the breastplate of justice.*

*"And your feet shod with the preparation of the gospel
of peace:*

*"In all things taking the shield of faith, where you
may be able to extinguish all the fiery darts of the most
wicked one.*

*"And take unto you the helmet of salvation, and the
sword of the Spirit (which is the word of God).*

*"By all prayer and supplication praying at all times in
the spirit; and in the same watching with all instance and
supplication for all the saints."* (Ephesians 6: 10–18)

≈§ Lord, help me to stand against the deceits of the
devil.

THE HOPEFUL SIDE OF THINGS

"You know, I think we give too much space in the press to the doings of freaks and crackpots and not enough to those of normal, decent people," a New York newspaper editor told a friend one day in his club. *"Why,"* he continued, *"in New York right now there must be hundreds of thousands of really good people . . . and what's more I'll bet a lot of them are saints and don't know it!"*

This incident calls to mind the answer someone once gave when asked the question: *"What makes the saints, saints?"* The reply given was revealing in its keen insight into human nature, rooted as it is in the divine. It went like this:

"Because they were Cheerful, when it was difficult to be Cheerful; Patient, when it was difficult to be Patient; They Pushed On, when they wanted to Stand Still; Kept Silence, when they wanted to Talk; Were Agreeable, when they wanted to be Disagreeable, That was All——

"It was quite simple. And always will be."

Once the millions of good people over the world—everyday "saints"—extend their goodness and become as energetic as the disciples of evil are in reaching out for all humanity, then this tired old earth of ours will be well on the high road to lasting peace.

"Much peace have they that love thy law, and to them there is no stumbling block." (Psalm 118:165)

⚜ Pray for the grace to carry Christ's love and truth to all men and not keep it selfishly to yourself.

PRAY FOR ALL

One of the easiest ways to grow in love of people—of all people—is to pray for them. Whether you are young or old, rich or poor, sick or well, in high position or low, possessed of many talents or few, prayer is a powerful means of helping the world. And it is always at your disposal.

Most people tend to restrict their prayers to their own immediate circle—very often to nothing beyond their own selfish interests. One lady in Washington, D.C., even requested that others pray that she *"win the Palmolive radio prize"!* Nothing wrong in that. We hope she won. But it would be better for her—and for everybody else—if she were also to pray for those who have never seen a radio: for the hundreds of millions who are wretchedly fed, housed, or clothed,—for the sick, the dying, the departed.

"Love thy neighbor as thyself" also means to pray for others as one does for oneself. . . . When you go to a movie, a ball game, the beach, into a train, a bus or street-car or into a crowd, say a brief prayer for *everyone* present. Eternity has begun for each of them, regardless of how little they know or think about it.

"Always in all my prayers making supplication for you all, with joy." (Philippians 1:4)

❧ Learn to pray frequently for others, especially those most in need of prayer.

REAL COURTESY

Early in the recent war a sauntering rookie soldier from Alabama encountered a brisk second lieutenant. *"Mawnin',"* drawled the rookie pleasantly.

The outraged officer launched a stinging lecture on military courtesy, with emphasis on saluting.

"Shucks," said the rookie, *"if I'da knowed you was gonna carry on like that, I wouldn't of spoke to you a-tall."*

The reaction of the rookie was natural enough. Most of us probably show routine courtesy to those we meet. But it is much more difficult to go out of one's way and be kind to those who are gruff in return.

Yet that should be the spirit of a Christopher—to make a special effort to be kind to those who least deserve it. More often than not, warmth and kindness, if pursued perseveringly, thaw out the frostiest of persons. In true charity, they supply what may be lacking in others.

"Let the charity of brotherhood abide in you." (Hebrews 13:1)

Pray that you may always be kind to those who fail in kindness to you.

THE COMMON TOUCH

Will Rogers once said, *"I never met a man I didn't like."*

All credit to him for that. In his varied life he met many people, all sorts of people, but he had the common touch that enabled him to see the good in everyone. People always liked him because he *first* liked them.

This natural disposition is a great gift of God. It becomes even greater when we proceed from natural love of those around us to supernatural love of those we don't meet, of all mankind. This is what Christ has asked of us, and this is the world's hope and our great opportunity.

"Love one another with brotherly affection, vying with one another in showing mutual regard." (Romans 12:10)

ᐁ Pray that you may have the gift of love for all mankind.

THE FOOL HATH SAID

Sometimes we think of atheism as a peculiarly modern invention, a product of science or materialism. But if we look into Scripture, we find that the prophets and Christ Himself spoke forcefully against those who deny their Creator.

1. *"The fool hath said in his heart: There is no God."* (Psalm 13:1)

2. *"But all men are vain, in whom there is not the knowledge of God: and who by these good things that are seen, could not understand him that is, neither by attending to the works have acknowledged who was the workman. . . . But then again they are not to be pardoned. For if they were able to know so much as to make a judgment of the world: how did they not more easily find out the Lord thereof?"* (Wisdom 13: 1; 8–9)

3. *"Thy own wickedness shall reprove thee, and thy apostasy shall rebuke thee. Know thou, and see that it is an evil and a bitter thing for thee, to have left the Lord thy God, and that my fear is not with thee, said the Lord the God of hosts."* (Jeremias 2:19)

4. *"But he that shall deny me before men, I will also deny him before my Father who is in heaven."* (Matthew 10:33)

⋖§ Pray that you may play an active role in spreading the knowledge and love of God.

ONLY THE BEGINNING

Entering the studio one morning, Charles Boyer was asked how he felt. He answered pleasantly, *"Slowly dying."*

"Why, Charles," said Loretta Young, *"what a gruesome thought."*

"Not at all," he replied, *"I began to die the day I was born."*

A lot of people take an unnatural attitude toward death, forgetting that the main reason they're alive is to get ready for their eternal life. It's like going to school: the most important event in a young person's education is commencement—the beginning of the life for which he has been prepared.

"For this corruptible body must needs put on incorruption; and this mortal body immortality. And when the mortal body shall have put on immortality, then shall come to pass the word which is written, Death is swallowed up in victory!" (I Corinthians 15:53-54)

ॐ Pray that you may be ever mindful of your eternal destiny.

WORTH REPEATING

Dante, that great-hearted, large-minded exemplar of all that was bright and good in medieval Christendom, once described the purpose of his writing in these beautiful words:

"... I am the man who, when Love lectures in the heart, takes notes, and then retells the lessons to the rest of men."

Whether we are writers, teachers, government employees, trade unionists, businessmen or wage-earners, housewives or students at school, we can—each one of us—reflect in our own relationships with others some small portion of the purpose and depth of understanding of the divine which made Dante the man he was.

We can listen to the lessons which the God Who is Love teaches us through religion and prayer, through friends, through nature, through books, and make it our most joyous aim in life to bring that lesson to others.

"... ask now the beasts, and they shall teach thee; and the birds of the air, and they shall tell thee. Speak to the earth, and it shall answer thee: and the fishes of the sea shall tell. Who is ignorant that the hand of the Lord hath made all these things?" (Job 12:7–9)

∜ Lord, teach me Thy lesson of love and enable me to retell it to the rest of men.

PRAY FOR YOUR GOVERNMENT

All of us, at one time or another, complain about our government. But how many of us actually *do* anything to make it better? In addition to our regular duties as citizens, we can give our government the very real benefit of our prayer. We can make up our own, or use the following Christopher prayer:

"Inspire us, O God, with such a deep love of our country that we will be actively concerned in its welfare as well as in that of all our fellow countrymen for time and for eternity. Teach us to show by word and deed the same zealous interest in protecting and furthering the Christian principles upon which our nation is founded that others display in belittling or eliminating them.

"Guide and strengthen the President, his Cabinet, the members of Congress, the delegates to the United Nations, the governor of our state, the officials of our community, and all others, in high position or low, who are entrusted with the task of protecting for all citizens those rights which come from Thee and from Thee alone.

"Teach us likewise to be worthy instruments in extending to all men of all nations, Thy children and our brothers, the same peace, freedom, and security with which Thou hast so abundantly blessed our land. Through Christ Our Lord. Amen."

WHAT'S IN A BOOK?

A friend of ours was complaining to his doctor that he "couldn't understand people." Shaking his head, he added, *"I've read all sorts of books on psychology, studied mental hygiene, taken a couple of years of 'psych' in college. I can't understand it; people simply puzzle me."*

The doctor answered at once, *"You're wasting your time trying to learn about human nature by reading books. You'll never understand people that way. You've got to live with people, work with them, mix with them. Books aren't the whole story. I find them useful chiefly as a guide to diagnosis."*

Some people make the mistake of trying to learn about God merely by reading books about Him. To understand Him, you've got to live with Him, work with Him, talk with Him. We do this in prayer. But we must not neglect to look for Him as He is reflected in our fellow men.

"God is not far from any one of us; for in Him we live and move and have our being . . . For we are His very offspring." (Acts 17:28)

&S O God, teach me to know Thee better by learning to love Thy image in all my fellow men.

JUST AS EASY

One day while St. Augustine was walking along the beach, pondering on the mystery of the Holy Trinity, he came across a child who had made a small hole in the sand and was running to the water with a little shell, filling it, then pouring the water into the hole. Puzzled, he stopped and asked the child what he was trying to do. The little boy answered, *"I'm pouring the ocean into this little hole."* St. Augustine then answered, *"Why, that's impossible."* To which the small boy replied, *"It's far easier for me to pour the ocean into this little hole, than for you to understand the mystery of the Holy Trinity."*

God wants us to use our minds upon everything in heaven and earth. No doubt about that. But He wants us also to remember that there are mysteries underpinning the whole structure of reality; that, try as we may—and ought—to fathom the depths, we shall never reach bottom. He who reverences the mysteries of life will, in large measure, avoid the shallowness of so many unhappy souls in our day.

"Who hath searched out the wisdom of God that goeth before all things?" (Ecclesiasticus 1:3)

&⸱ O Lord, I believe, help Thou my unbelief.

A NEEDED WARNING

On Armistice Day we might all think over a speech of General Omar Bradley, our Army's Chief of Staff. Speaking in Boston, on November 10, 1948, the distinguished military leader warned:

"With the monstrous weapons man already has, humanity is in danger of being trapped in this world by its moral adolescents. Our knowledge of science has clearly outstripped our capacity to control it. We have many men of science, but too few men of God. We have grasped the mystery of the atom and rejected the Sermon on the Mount. Man is stumbling blindly through a spiritual darkness while toying with the precarious secrets of life and death.

"The world has achieved brilliance without wisdom, power without conscience. Ours is a world of nuclear giants and ethical infants. We know more about war than we know about peace, more about killing than we know about living. This is our twentieth century's claim to distinction and to progress."

"The wisdom of the flesh is death; but the wisdom of the spirit is life and peace." (Roman 8:6)

&ξ O Lord, bestow on me the grace to be an instrument of Thy peace.

PAUSE FOR REFLECTION

A policeman pounding his beat one night stopped at the alley door of a servicemen's club. To his surprise the door opened.

Staring at him, he said, was a *"big, burly man, ready to jump me."*

He drew his gun. The prowler drew his. They both fired. A full-length mirror and the prowler—the policeman's reflection—crashed to the floor.

This kind of mistake has happened to most of us, but how many of us have ever stopped to think of the significance of it? How often have troubles seemed to loom large and menacing, then when we face them courageously, we find they disappear, insignificant as shadows in a broken mirror? When we feel that there's nothing we can do, then it's time for us to realize that the best thing we can do is to seek God's help and then face the situation for what it is: turn on the light, rather than fear the "ghost" in the darkness.

"For I am the Lord thy God who take thee by the hand, and say to thee: Fear not, I have helped thee." (Isaias 41:13)

> Pray for the fearless confidence that comes from trust in God.

THE TWO HOUSES

A father and his five-year-old son were walking along a street in Jamaica, Long Island. Suddenly the little boy said, *"Look, Daddy, what an old ramshackle house!"*

The father seized the opportunity to teach his son a lesson in personal responsibility. *"Yes, it certainly is, son. See how dirty it is, how the shutters look as though they're about to fall off, how the floor boards on the porch are all rotted. Now, do you remember the lovely Rufus King house I showed you the other day? That house was built long before this—way back before Washington was our first president, in fact. Yet the Rufus King house is in very good condition . . . and do you know why? Because people have taken care of it these past two hundred years, while the people who lived in this house neglected it."*

A Christopher will ever try to shoulder his full share of the responsibility for the salvation and peace of the world. He will not allow unconcern and neglect to contribute to the trend toward spiritual decay any more than he will avoid his material obligations to his fellow man.

". . . and the ruin of that house was great." (Luke 6:49)

Pray that you may ever keep alive in yourself and in others the sense of personal responsibility.

WHEN THAT DAY COMES

"We hate Christianity and Christians. Even the best of them must be considered our worst enemies. They preach love of one's neighbor and mercy, which is contrary to our principles. What we want is hate. . . . Only then will we conquer the Universe."

These are the words of Anatole Lunacharsky, Soviet Commissar of Education, quoted in *Izvestia*. They point out an important fact: the one thing that terrifies the godless the world over is the fear that someday all those who believe in Christ will wake up—*and start acting their beliefs.*

Once that happens, most of the great problems which plague mankind will disappear overnight. That is the goal toward which all Christophers are working.

"So faith also, if it have not works, is dead in itself." (James 2:17)

❧ Pray that you may not only believe but act also.

NO MAN IS AN ISLAND

It's hard for any of us to realize that any time another suffers, we also are affected. But if we are true to our Christian belief, this is exactly the case. As John Donne, the famous poet, wrote several hundred years ago:

"The Church is Catholic, universal; so are all her actions. All that she does belongs to all. When she baptizes a child, that action concerns me. All mankind is of one Author. . . . No man is an island, entire of itself. Every man is a piece of the continent, a part of the main. If a clod be washed away by the sea, Europe is the less. . . . Any man's death diminishes me, because I am involved in mankind."

Many people today have a "leave-me-alone" point of view; they don't want to "get involved" in anything. But the fact of the matter is that they are, as Donne says, *"involved in mankind."* When they realize this and act in harmony with their fellow men, they begin to live more fully.

"We many are one body in Christ and members each of the other." (Romans 12:5)

❧ Let me not be wise in my own conceit. Give me to be of one mind with all men of good will.

PASSION FOR GOLD

Reviewing two recent books on the California gold rush, *Time* magazine commented:

"Together they give an unforgettable impression of a mighty movement of people, unorganized and yet queerly efficient, undisciplined and yet tenacious, unbeatable, ignorant, misled, unprepared, unaided, persisting despite almost every obstacle."

This tremendous movement of people from all over the nation to the West is one of the most stirring passages in all our history. Yet—the driving purpose behind this "push" was a passion for gold.

If only those who already possess the treasure of truth would strive as vigorously to share their treasure with the world, what a difference it would make in every phase of our life today!

"Do not lay up for yourselves treasures upon the earth, where moth and rust consume, and where thieves break through and steal. . . . For where thy treasure is, there will thy heart be also." (Matthew 6:19, 21)

≥§ Lord, give me the driving purpose that will enable me to bring Thee to others.

THEY DID IT BEFORE

Outstanding among all countries is the missionary zeal of Ireland. Down through the centuries she considered it a great privilege to send out messengers of the Prince of Peace to every corner of the world. Of her great achievements from the sixth to the ninth century one historian wrote:

"At a time when godless hordes of barbarians threatened to blot out Christianity from the face of the Continent, the green isle away in the western seas became the refuge and the home of religion and the nursery of long generations of saints and apostles, who went forth in their day, carrying the glad Gospel tidings once more to those regions where the wars of centuries had darkened or wholly extinguished the light of the true faith of Christ."

In our generation, it may well be that Providence has given America the *mission* of playing a tremendous part in bringing the faith and love of Christ to the whole world. And you can play a personal role in this. *You* can change the world.

"You are the light of the world. So let your light shine before men that they may see your good works and glorify your Father, Who is in Heaven." (Matthew 5: 14–16)

⤳ Pray for the hundreds of millions who have yet to hear of Christ.

THE MORE WE GIVE

While in Milan some time ago I tried to find someone who spoke English. Finally, a young couple was pointed out to me, with the suggestion that perhaps they might be able to help me.

"*I speak English, though not much,*" the girl volunteered in answer to my question. "*But I'm teaching it to Carlo here*"—she indicated her companion. "*I find the best way to learn English myself is to teach it to someone else.*"

It was worth the trip to Milan just to hear this one remark which expresses so well an important Christopher idea: *the more we give the more we get.* In the truest sense, one of the best ways to keep one's faith is to "*give it away.*" On the other hand, one of the easiest ways to lose one's faith is to "*keep it to one's self.*"

"*Silver and gold I have none; but what I have, I give thee. . . .*" (Acts 3:6)

⋅⋅⋅ Pray that even those who have some little glimmer of the Truth may share it with those who have none.

IF HE ONLY KNEW

An architect who had worked for a large corporation for many years was called in one day by the board of directors and given plans for a model house to be built in the most exclusive residential section of the city. The chairman instructed him to spare no expense, to use the finest materials and the best labor available.

As the work progressed, the architect began to think: *"No one will ever know what goes into the unseen parts. Why hire such expensive labor? Why use such costly materials?"* He began to substitute inferior materials, to hire inferior labor, pocketing the difference.

Shortly after the house was finished, the chairman of the board held a reception to celebrate its completion. After making a lengthy speech, he amazed the architect by presenting him with the keys to the house: *"We give you this house,"* he said, *"as a token of the high esteem we have for your many years of splendid and faithful service."*

"For what things a man shall sow, those also shall he reap." (Galatians 6:8)

⇛ Pray that this important lesson may be ever present in your own mind and that God may teach it to many others.

323

THE TRAINING TABLE

Everyone knows about training tables. There, according to the season, dine the members of football, wrestling, boxing, and rowing teams. A special diet is prepared for each, according to his needs. Sweets are out. They make fat. Muscle and bone-building foods are in. Down one side of the room, to those not in training, float the trays with roast pork, gravy, dressing, apple pie, coffee with cream and sugar. But to the tables of those in training go: lean and not too tender beef, green vegetables, salads, fruit, and milk.

Many a boy hates this sort of diet, but hangs on though the tantalizing fragrance of favorite foods fills the air. Why does he stand for it? He's been told he must if he wants to be on the varsity.

Followers of Christ work at self-restraint and discipline to strengthen their spiritual fiber. They give up many attractive things. They don't want fatty tissues of self-indulgence to slow them up. They're in a contest for eternal victory.

"Every competitor restraineth himself in all things— they, to be sure, to receive a perishable crown, but we an imperishable." (I Corinthians 9:25)

&ξ Lord, teach me the wisdom of self-discipline.

EVERYBODY CAN DO SOMETHING

You've probably heard the old axiom that *"you can't give what you haven't got."* Nobody should, however, mistake this to mean that, if he is not a spiritual expert, he can't do anything for anyone else in a spiritual way. There's not a person in the world who can't give something to the betterment of the world. No matter how far removed from God one may be, he remains a child of God by creation, and so can still do something *for* God, thereby coming at least one degree closer to his Maker.

It is also true that one who would play a special role, that of a zealous Christopher, must make an extra effort to develop his interior life and increase his spiritual power, not simply for his own self-sanctification but for the sanctification of the *world*.

The more one prays, the more one grows in the knowledge and love of God, and therefore he the more effectively brings Him into the world.

"For consider your call, brethren; not many of you are learned in a worldly sense, not many in high station, not many well-born. On the contrary, God chose the simple things of the world to confound the learned; and God chose the weak things of the world to confound the powerful . . ." (I Corinthians 1: 26–27)

Pray for the courage to give and keep giving, no matter how little you have to give.

SHE PLAYED HER PART

To one who expressed sympathy to Countess Bernadotte after the tragic death of her husband in the Holy Land, the Countess replied:

"I am proud of my husband. I knew all the time that he was taking many great risks. But we always felt it would be better to take risks serving one's fellow man for the love of God than live to ninety and simply rust out. And so each time I gladly encouraged him to go. It gave me a great thrill one day to have my wonderful husband say to me, 'It does help me so much to know you are not holding me back.' In this way I felt I was playing a little part in the great work he was doing."

To concern ourselves with the welfare—spiritual as well as material—of others often requires great sacrifice which we must be willing to bear for the love of God and His honor and glory. Sometimes, of course, your role in this Christlike work may only be one of encouragement and assistance to others to get into the "thick of things" rather than active, direct participation. But no matter the part we play, it should be with all our heart and all our mind and all our strength. For a Christopher, especially, this should be the crowning purpose of life.

"Greater love than this no man hath, that a man lay down his life for his friends." (John 15:13)

᪷ Pray that you may learn to sacrifice yourself and encourage others to do great things.

IN GRATITUDE

In Seattle on November 22, 1945, General Jonathan Wainwright offered the following Thanksgiving prayer. The words he spoke that first postwar Thanksgiving are still worth repeating:

"Oh, God, our Father, today we give Thee thanks for the things we take for granted, for freedom, for security of life, for food and shelter, and the presence of loved ones. . . .

"We thank Thee that once again men may have hope, opportunity to work and plan for a better future, a chance to secure peace, and an ampler life for themselves and their children.

"Keep us humble in the day of victory, make us wise in the presence of great problems, strong and brave in the face of any danger, and sympathetic and generous as we face the appalling need of a war-torn world.

"In gratitude for all those who paid the price of victory we now ask Thy guidance as we dedicate ourselves to that cause for which they gave their last whole measure of devotion. Lord of Hosts, be with us yet, lest we forget! Amen."

"For all these things bless the Lord that made thee . . ." (Ecclesiasticus 32:17)

ᴥᔤ Thanks be to God our Father, through Jesus Christ our Redeemer, for all His blessings.

327

THANKS BY DOING

Abraham Lincoln said many things that provoke deep thought and inspire to great deeds. One of his most thoughtful utterances is worthy of serious attention:

"We have been the recipients of the choicest bounties of heaven; we have been preserved these many years in peace and prosperity; we have grown in numbers, wealth, and power as no other nation has ever grown.

"But we have forgotten God. We have forgotten the gracious hand which preserved us in peace and multiplied and enriched and strengthened us, and we have vainly imagined, in the deceitfulness of our hearts, that all these things were produced by some superior wisdom and virtue of our own.

"Intoxicated with unbroken success, we have become too self-sufficient to feel the necessity of redeeming and preserving grace, too proud to pray to the God that made us."

It would be a sure sign of our gratitude to God for His blessings on our country, if tens of thousands of young Americans would dedicate themselves to preserving our precious heritage of God-given abundance and freedom; and would then go out "over the earth" to share these "choicest bounties" with the rest of mankind.

Freely have you received, freely give. (Matthew 10:8)

"Go into the whole world and preach the gospel to every creature." (Mark 16:15)

꡴ Pray the Lord to send thousands of young people into the market place to bring His blessings to others.

THE SPHERES THAT COUNT

If you stop and reflect for a moment you will probably agree that the great majority of the best citizens in every community, those with the best sense of values, are engaged in pursuits or professions *that have little purpose beyond earning a living.* They are seldom found in occupations that are concerned with the formation of thought or the leadership of people. More often than not they are merchants or elevator operators, manufacturers or salesmen, bakers or engineers, barbers or railroad executives.

Good people are needed in every walk of life, but particularly in the spheres that influence millions. A refreshing change for the better will come only when enough people with high quality and purpose also make it their business to go as Christophers into education, government, writing, trade unions, social service, and libraries. Once they bring to bear the tremendous influence over the minds and hearts of men that people in such positions wield, more and more people with a Christopher purpose will strive to take active roles in these same influential spheres.

"And he said to them: Go you also into my vineyard." (Matthew 20:4)

Pray for the grace to make of your life what God wishes it to be—a service to all mankind.

THE GENTLEMAN

Cardinal Newman in his book *Idea of a University,* has one section entitled, "Man of the World," and in it he sets forth his views on the various qualities which go to make up a gentleman. As he observes:

". . . It is almost a definition of a gentleman to say he is one who never inflicts pain.

". . . The true gentleman . . . carefully avoids whatever may cause a jar or jolt in the minds of those with whom he is cast—all clashing of opinion, or collision of feeling, all restraint, or suspicion, or gloom, or resentment; his great concern being to make every one at their ease and at home.

"He has eyes on all his company; he is tender towards the bashful, gentle towards the distant, and merciful towards the absurd; he can recollect to whom he is speaking; he guards against unseasonable allusions, or topics which may irritate; he is seldom prominent in conversation, and never wearisome.

"He makes light of favours while he does them, and seems to be receiving when he is conferring.

"He never speaks of himself except when compelled, never defends himself by a mere retort, he has no ears for slander or gossip, is scrupulous in imputing motives to those who interfere with him, and interprets everything for the best."

(*continued tomorrow*)

⋙ Pray for the patience to be ever courteous.

THE GENTLEMAN (*continued*)

"He is never mean or little in his disputes, never takes unfair advantage, never mistakes personalities or sharp sayings for arguments, or insinuates evil which he dare not say out.

"From a long-sighted prudence, he observes the maxim of the ancient sage, that we should ever conduct ourselves towards our enemy as if he were one day to be our friend. . . .

"If he engages in controversy of any kind, his disciplined intellect preserves him from the blundering discourtesy of better though less educated minds; who, like blunt weapons, tear and hack instead of cutting clean, who mistake the point in argument, waste their strength on trifles, misconceive their adversary, and leave the question more involved than they find it.

"He may be right or wrong in his opinion, but he is too clear-headed to be unjust; he is as simple as he is forcible, and as brief as he is decisive."

Remembering always the qualities that are expected of a gentleman, we would do well to be conscious also that the deepest motivation must ever be the love of Christ and our neighbor, not mere pagan love of self.

"A man of understanding is faithful to the law of God, and the law is faithful to him." (Ecclesiasticus 33:3)

❧ O Lord, let me learn and relearn the wisdom of doing unto others as I would have them do unto me.

GIVE TILL IT HURTS

During the depression a charitable organization which raised funds partly through the sale of "scrap" received a large box of lead foil. It was weighed and found to be worth exactly $1.80.

One of the workers in smoothing out a piece of the foil was amused to see that it came from the top of a champagne bottle.

She unrolled another piece and saw it was the same. Finally she unrolled every piece in the box and discovered they were all from the same source—the necks of champagne bottles!

The donor of the lead foil probably regarded the gift as a true act of charity. But how often we limit our giving to mere "leftovers"! The true spirit of charity involves a personal sacrifice; the greatest gift is a part of ourselves.

"I was an eye to the blind and a foot to the lame." (Job 29:15)

⋙ Lord, teach me to be as generous with others as Thou art with me.

ONE SMALL VOICE

A sixteen-year-old Chicago girl recently wrote a letter to a magazine publisher, pointing out in a friendly, constructive manner the harm she felt the magazine was doing, among young people particularly, by its selection and presentation of subjects.

Not long afterward she received a reply from the publisher, expressing appreciation for her thoughtful interest and her sympathetic, positive approach. He suggested she go over the next issue, article by article, adding a brief criticism of each.

The girl gladly complied. Soon a second letter reached her from the publisher, enclosing a check for $25 for *"her service"* and with the much more rewarding news that her observations had inspired several office memoranda on editorial policy.

God blessed the little effort of that sixteen-year-old girl in Chicago to *"reach for the world."* Because she took the time and trouble to *"make her voice heard"* in an effort to make things better, she succeeded in bringing about some improvement at least in articles that are read by millions.

"The voice of one crying in the wilderness: prepare ye the way of the Lord." (Matthew 3:3)

❧ Pray that you will look for opportunities to bring God's truth into the midst of the market place.

COLLECT FOR WHAT?

A rare collection of bronzes was auctioned off a few years ago in New York. The collection was one of the best in the world. The owner had spent twenty-five years of care and more than a million dollars in gathering it. The one and only heir, his wife, was bequeathed thousands of bronzes which meant nothing to her; she much preferred a modest collection of greenbacks. With well-trained indifference the auctioneer sold the two hundred lots, scattering the work of a lifetime in a few hours and for a fraction of their worth.

So many of the things on which we lavish our energy, laudable as they may be in themselves, are often scattered at our death as easily as a child's wooden blocks. It seems good sense then, instead of playing with the wooden blocks of this life, to lay up indestructible treasures in the next.

"But lay up to yourselves treasures in heaven: where neither rust nor moth can consume, and where thieves do not break through and steal." (Matthew 6:20)

◈ Pray that you may always remember where your true treasure lies . . . with Christ for all eternity.

ON TACKLING TROUBLE

With the practical wisdom so characteristic of many colored people, Bessie, a good-natured cook who had cheerfully weathered many a storm of her own, was giving a bit of sound advice to the lady of the house on how to meet trouble. Said Bessie:

"I've tried going round trouble. I've tried going over it. I've tried going under it. But it's no use. I find the best way to tackle trouble is to plow right through it!"

Time and again we all learn through sad experience that dodging difficulties we should bravely "tackle" only means facing bigger ones later. Centuries ago the author of the *Imitation of Christ* wrote:

"Thou canst not escape it (the cross), whithersoever thou runnest; for whithersoever thou goest, thou carriest thyself with thee, and shalt always find thyself.

"Turn thyself upwards, or turn thyself downwards, turn thyself without or turn thyself within thee, and everywhere thou shalt find the cross . . .

"If thou carry the cross willingly, it will carry thee, and bring thee to thy desired end: to wit, to that place where there will be an end of suffering, though here there will be none.

"If thou carriest it unwillingly, thou makest it a burden to thee . . . If thou fling away one cross without doubt thou wilt find another, and perhaps a heavier." (Imitation, Bk. 2, Ch. 12; 4–5)

⋙ O God, give me the good sense to see the wisdom of cheerfully *taking up* my cross daily, not waiting for it to be thrust on me.

UNDER HIS FEET

A homesteader in Texas, suffering financial difficulties, came to the conclusion that he ought to move on to California, where he *"could really make some money."* He had difficulty getting rid of his property and finally sold it for a very small sum. Shortly after taking over, the new tenant discovered oil on his land. Within a few short months he became a millionaire.

The farmer had been looking far away for assistance. Yet all the time the solution to all his financial problems lay right under his feet.

Sometimes our very familiarity with the things around us blinds us to their real worth. We think to find our opportunities to do things for God, for example, in some unusual position where we can do extraordinary things. Yet all the while in the humdrum of our daily tasks we have all the opportunities we need to start bringing the love of God to our fellow men.

"Jesus therefore said to him, Unless you see signs and wonders, you do not believe." (John 4:48)

&§ Lord, help me to see my opportunities to start reaching for the world in my everyday tasks.

THE MOTIVE COUNTS

At one of last season's most elaborate debuts the wealthy matron responsible for it beamed in triumph. Her months of careful preparation and the money she'd spent on it— some $20,000—were being well rewarded. Guest after guest, fortified with an abundance of champagne, rushed up to her and gushed, *"This is the party of parties!"* or *"I've never seen anything like it before!"* Meanwhile, the person for whom the affair was actually given, the matron's daughter, was little more than a figurehead in all the festivities.

Later, she regretfully remarked to a friend: *"My mother didn't give that party for me. She gave it for herself. I was only the excuse!"*

All of us are in constant danger of getting our motives mixed. The Devil makes it his business to see that we do. Even the most charitable of works can be used as an "excuse" to further one's personal ambitions. And many use a good cause for their private advantage. They go into government, for instance, to "take out," not to "put in." Their object is not to do good for others, but *to do well for themselves.*

 Pray that you may perform all your good works, not for self-aggrandizement, but for the benefit of your fellows and the greater glory of God.

EXPECT TROUBLE

If you meet a lot of bumps and obstacles playing the role of a Christopher, it is a good sign that the *"Lord is with you."* If things come *too easy*, then it is time to worry a bit!

To anyone who would be a Christ-bearer, Christ promised not a path strewn with roses, but hardship, misunderstanding, and a share of the same suffering that was His lot from the crib to the cross. Every Christopher should remember these words of His:

1. *If any man will come after me, let him deny himself, and take up his cross daily, and follow me."* (Luke 9:23)

2. *If the world hate you, know ye that it hath hated me before you."* (John 15:18)

3. *"He that findeth his life shall lose it; and he that shall lose his life for me, shall find it."* (Matthew 10:39)

⋑ Pray that you will learn to expect difficulties; and pray also that you will acquire the strength to meet them when they come.

LET'S FACE IT

On the cheerful acceptance of trouble, the author of the *Imitation of Christ* continues:

"Dost thou think to escape that which no mortal could ever avoid? What saint was there ever in the world without his cross and affliction?

"Our Lord Jesus Christ Himself was not one hour of His life without suffering: 'It behooveth,' saith He, 'that Christ should suffer and rise from the dead, and so enter His glory' (Luke 24, 46). And how dost thou pretend to seek another way than this royal way, which is the way of the holy cross?

"The whole life of Christ was a cross and a martyrdom; and dost thou seek rest and joy? Thou errest, thou errest, if thou seekest any other thing than to suffer tribulations; for this whole mortal life is full of miseries, and beset on all sides with crosses.

"And the higher a person is advanced in spirit, the heavier crosses shall he often meet with, because the pain of his banishment increases in proportion to his love.

". . . And the flesh is brought down by affliction, the more the spirit is strengthened by inward grace." (Imitation, Bk. 2, Ch. 12, 6–8)

⋍§ Pray that you may have the courage to love others all the way.

"THE BEST SHE COULD"

A Rhode Island farmer had the following words carved on the headstone of his wife's grave:

"She did the best she could."

In a way, this might seem a bit dubious. Yet in a true sense it is high tribute to anyone. If it can be truthfully said of each of us, when God calls us, that "he did the best he could" to make the world a bit the better for his being in it—that would be tribute enough before God and man.

Christ does not demand the impossible of any of us. He does want us to do the best we can with the talents with which he has entrusted us.

However, if we bury the talents He has given us, if we insist on hiding our light under a bushel, if we postpone, neglect, avoid, or otherwise fail to play our part, however small, in "changing the world for the better," then it might be more truthful if it were written about us: *"He failed to do the best he could."*

". . . unless your justice abound more than that of the scribes and Pharisees, you shall not enter into the kingdom of heaven." (Matthew 5:20)

⁀§ Pray to use every opportunity to show the same care for others that you show for yourself.

FOR GOOD, NOT EVIL

Someone once said that *"thoughtless, catty remarks about others have probably created more unnecessary enemies than any other form of human relationship."*

A Christopher above all others should take particular pains to see that his tongue is used for good, never for evil; to console, not to condemn; to build up, not to tear down; to rejoice at the good fortune of others, never to begrudge them success.

Though seldom admitted, gossip is one of the most dangerous of sins. Sometimes it may amount to nothing more than a seemingly harmless word, maybe nothing more than a slight inflection, yet the effect is often deadly—and permanent. A reputation can easily be damaged or even killed in a matter of moments. And without a chance for one word of defense on the part of the person misrepresented.

Even if the fault of another is true—and known—gossip about it serves no useful purpose and is sinful. To offer a charitable word of mercy, of excuse, of forgiveness is the Christlike approach.

"By this will all men know that you are my disciples, if you have love for one another." (John 13:35)

꿈 Teach me, O Lord, to encourage the good in others, not to be a fault-finder.

THE TONGUE

One of the most stirring references to the tongue to be found anywhere is that of the Apostle St. James, the first Bishop of Jerusalem:

"For in many things we all offend. If any man offend not in word, the same is a perfect man. He is able also with a bridle to lead about the whole body.

"For if we put bits into the mouths of horses, that they may obey us, and we turn about their whole body.

"Behold also ships, whereas they are great, and are driven by strong winds, yet are they turned about with a small helm, whithersoever the force of the governor willeth.

"Even so the tongue is indeed a little member, and boasteth great things. Behold how small a fire kindleth a great wood.

"And the tongue is a fire, a world of iniquity. The tongue is placed among our members, which defileth the whole body, and inflameth the wheel of our nativity, being set on fire by hell.

"For every nature of beasts, and of birds, and of serpents, and of the rest, is tamed, and hath been tamed, by the nature of man:

"But the tongue no man can tame, an unquiet evil, full of deadly poison.

"By it we bless God and the Father: and by it we curse men, who are made after the likeness of God.

"Out of the same mouth proceedeth blessing and cursing. My brethren, these things ought not so to be." (James 3:2–10)

◄§ Pray that you may guard your tongue as jealously as the innermost secrets of your heart.

WIN PEOPLE, NOT ARGUMENTS

Not long ago a young businessman left a very important conference after engaging for more than an hour in a heated debate over policy. As he entered his own office, he muttered in a boastful tone to his secretary, *"Well, I guess I won that argument!"*

Personal triumph seems to have been the source of this young man's happiness. He seems to have been less interested in helping others to see the truth than in pushing himself. His was the shallow *"pride of being right,"* not the joy of helping others better to understand the truth.

The true Christopher is far less interested in winning a debate, in forcing someone to admit defeat, than in helping him to arrive at the truth. One seldom wins persons by argument, but only by love, which aims at supplying what may be lacking in others.

"Death and life are in the power of the tongue: they that love it, shall eat the fruits thereof." (Proverbs 18:21)

❧ Lord, take from me the "pride of being right," and give me the love of sharing with others the truth Thou hast entrusted to me.

343

MOST SPECIFIC

Many who either know little of Christ, or who take out of His teaching only what they like, tend to gloss over the positive, specific *"laying down of the law"* which is plainly evident throughout the Gospels.

Never once does Christ force acceptance of His truth. He leaves each person free to accept or reject His teachings. On the other hand, never once does He "water down" the truth, compromise, or give the idea that anyone is free to believe "whatever he likes." He says, in effect, *"take it or leave it, but don't forget the consequences"*

1. *"Amen, amen, I say to thee, unless a man be born again of water and the Spirit, he cannot enter into the kingdom of God."* (John 3:5)

2. *"Amen, amen, I say to you, unless you eat the flesh of the Son of Man, and drink his blood, you shall not have life in you."* (John 6:54)

3. *"If you love me, keep my commandments."* (John 14:15)

4. *"But whoever disowns me before men, I in turn will disown him before my Father in heaven."* (Matthew 10:33)

5. *". . . without me you can do nothing."* (John 15:5)

And that no one might doubt His authority to command adherence to His teachings, He said without the slightest reservation:

6. *"All power in heaven and on earth hath been given me. Go ye, therefore, teach all nations. Teach them to observe all that I have commanded you. Behold, I am with you all days, unto the consummation of the world."* (Matthew 28:18-20)

❧ Lord, I believe: help thou mine unbelief!

344

A BIG DIFFERENCE

One day a small boy was trying to lift a heavy stone, but he couldn't budge it. His father, passing by, stopped to watch his efforts. Finally he said to his son: *"Are you using all your strength?"*

"Yes, I am," the boy cried, exasperated.

"No," the father said calmly, *"you're not. You haven't asked me to help you."*

How often we give up when the job seems beyond our limited capacities! And yet we cannot estimate our ability properly, unless we include the immeasurable resources at our disposal when we co-operate with the help of God. When we are attempting a task—big or small—we would do well to stop for a moment and pray, in all humility, for God's help. This is a fitting reminder of our dependence on God, as well as an assurance of help from on high that will carry us through difficulties we could never master alone.

". . . for the hand of the Lord was with me, strengthening me." (Ezechiel 3:14)

⊷ Our help is in the name of the Lord, who made Heaven and earth.

A FIERCE WARNING

In his epistle to the early Romans, Paul lashed out at those who refused to acknowledge God. In his fierce warning we can find much that applies to our own time.

"Because that, when they knew God, they have not glorified him as God, or given thanks; but became vain in their thoughts, and their foolish heart was darkened.

"For professing themselves to be wise, they became fools.

"And they changed the glory of the incorruptible God into the likeness of the image of a corruptible man, and of birds, and of fourfooted beasts, and of creeping things.

"Wherefore God gave them up to the desires of their heart, unto uncleanness, to dishonour their own bodies among themselves:

"Who changed the truth of God into a lie; and worshiped and served the creature rather than the Creator, who is blessed for ever. Amen." (Romans 1:21-25)

(continued tomorrow)

⏜ Pray that you will never flinch where the honor of God is at stake.

A FIERCE WARNING (*continued*)

Paul continues his detailed reproval of the Romans, who, rejecting God, fell into the mire of their own depravity.

"*For this cause God delivered them up to shameful affections . . .*

"*And as they liked not to have God in their knowledge, God delivered them up to a reprobate sense, to do those things which are not proper.*

"*Being filled with all iniquity, malice, fornication, avarice, wickedness, full of envy, murder, contention, deceit, malignity, whisperers.*

"*Detractors, hateful to God, contumelious, proud, haughty, inventors of evil things, disobedient to parents.*

"*Foolish, dissolute, without affection, without fidelity, without mercy:*

"*Who, having known the justice of God, did not understand that they who do such things are worthy of death, and not only they that do them, but they also that consent to them that do them.*" (Romans 1:26–32)

⍻ O God, I thank Thee for the grace of following Thee instead of my own weak inclinations.

347

A SIGNIFICANT DISTINCTION

Arnold Lunn once wrote that there are two kinds of democracy, making a distinction that gives us much food for reflection. There is, as he put it, the democracy of the saint, which is based on compassion and humility and says, *"You're as good as I am."* Opposed to that is the democracy of the sinner, which is based on envy and has as its slogan: *"I'm as good as you are."*

The words of these two mottoes are similar, but what a difference there is in the meaning. If we believe in an abstract principle like democracy, we can best show what we believe by our actions. A man who does nothing is likely to believe in nothing; a man with an important idea will be inspired by that idea. Our democracy wasn't built by the lazy or the indifferent.

". . . three things . . . approved before God and men: The concord of brethren, and the love of neighbors, and man and wife that agree well together." (Ecclesiasticus 25:1, 2)

Help me, Lord, never to fall prey to the easy way of indifference; but grant that I may ever choose the harder way of continual effort for good.

348

TAKE PEOPLE AS THEY ARE

The Gospels make it clear that Christ took men as they were and built on the raw material offered Him. To a chosen few He gave special training and instruction to equip them to be full-fledged, fully-accredited apostles. Yet He wished every person who had even the smallest consciousness of His truth to participate actively in spreading it.

He was willing to accept co-operation from any well-meaning source, and, in so doing, He occasionally ran counter to His disciples.

They were obviously proud of themselves when, one day, they told Him that a certain man was *"casting out devils in Thy name, and we forbade him, because he followeth not with us."* But Christ corrected them: *"Forbid him not; for he that is not against you, is for you."* (Luke 9:49–50)

Encouraging the person farthest from Christ to say one prayer or do one thing for Christ usually results in his coming one step closer to Christ.

⋙ Pray that you may be able to see and encourage the possibilities for good in others, no matter who or what they are.

START THEM YOUNG

A friend of ours, walking home from work one evening, experienced a genuine thrill when she saw, scrawled on a fence in a childish hand in large letters, the words: *"I love God."* What made the incident more inspiring was the fact that this expression of affection for the Creator of all was sandwiched in between scores of obscene sentiments which literally cluttered the fence from top to bottom.

Even a small child can be inspired to spread the love of God to everyone as far as he can reach. Christ at the age of twelve, you remember, said to His Mother: *". . . I must be about my Father's business."* (Luke 2:49)

A child, too, can be guided into thinking of investing his whole life in the business of spreading Christ's love in the market place through a career in one of the four fields of influence—*education, government, labor relations, and writing*—into a life's work where he can do more than merely make a living.

"Let the little children come to me, and do not hinder them, for of such is the kingdom of God." (Luke 18:16)

◄§ Pray that you may influence many young persons to devote their lives to the work of spreading God's truth.

WHICH DIRECTION?

In an English churchyard the following epitaph is carved on one of the ancient headstones:

"Remember, man that passeth by,
As thou art now, so once was I;
And as I am so thou must be;
Prepare thyself to follow me."

Some visitor with a sense of discrimination scribbled the following underneath:

"To follow thee's not my intent,
—Unless I know which way thou went."

It's easy to wander through life aimlessly, seldom giving any thought to the fact that the ultimate destination for each of us is either Heaven or Hell.

Where each of us goes depends on where he *wants* to go.

On what we do, or fail to do, over a lifetime for the love of God and others, as well as for ourselves, depends our eternal destination.

"But he that shall persevere to the end, he shall be saved." (Matthew 24:13)

&ampamp;§ Pray that you may be ever conscious of your eternal destiny.

SHUNNING RESPONSIBILITY

Those who would work most effectively for good will make every effort to become more efficient in their work. To this end one habit of which it would be well to rid oneself is *indecision*. Many otherwise excellent persons frequently suffer from this defect. Of course one must always know the goal he is pursuing before he can act at all. Legitimate deliberation is sound. But indecision is deliberation unduly prolonged.

Those who have studied the problem of indecision have made a significant discovery: No matter how long the period of deliberation may be, *"no new thought turns up after the first five or ten minutes of reflection. Lack of decision means ultimately shunning responsibility."*

Finally, those who cannot decide are really egotistic: *"They wish to avoid any mistake whatever; they want, in fact, to be found absolutely faultless."* If we remember the words, "The man who never made a mistake never made anything," we will be less apt to think we can expect to be perfect in every thing we do.

"In all thy works be quick. . . ." (Ecclesiasticus 31:27)

◄§ Pray that you may never allow the theoretical *best* to be the enemy of the practical *better*.

352

IN SOCIAL WORK

For many people the only source of human rights is society itself. Therefore, they believe that what society can give, society can take away. They forget—or conveniently ignore—the fact that the source of all natural rights is *God*. This ignorance, or oversight, is brought into exceptionally sharp focus in the *field of social work*. So tremendous is this field, and so great its potentialities for good or evil, that it is encouraging to know that many in this work are struggling to uphold the basic truths upon which our nation was founded. Not long ago Jane Hoey, director of the Federal Bureau of Public Assistance, Social Security Board, pointed out:

"Belief in the divine origin and destiny of man and recognition of the Godlike quality common to all men should provide the incentive necessary to conquer prejudice, to develop self-discipline, and to control actions that interfere with the rights of others.

"Such belief and recognition should likewise inspire continuous service to humanity. . . . Social work is vitalized by the concept that service to individuals is given on the basis of kinship to God and the recipient."

The Christopher who has this clear-cut concept of the divine origin and destiny of man can do much in the field of social work to insure more lasting blessings to many here, and over the world, who are finding the battle of life ever more difficult.

⋅≼ Pray that God will send thousands, who believe in the divine origin and destiny of man, into the field of social work.

353

BEFORE THE VERDICT

In a murder trial in Colorado last year the jury gave the nation a stirring example of its sense of responsibility. When the trial was over, the foreman of the twelve-man panel announced that before reaching a verdict the group had said this prayer:

"Almighty God, help us in this hour of deliberation. Give us wisdom that we may be guided to a just and fair verdict to all concerned. Let Thy spirit descend upon us so that our conscience will become Thy will. With malice towards none and forethought of the duty we are about to perform, let us, Thy mortals, have divine guidance in this deliberation. Amen."

This is a heartening sign. When more men in positions of responsibility show in this *public* way their dependence upon God, there cannot help being a great change for the better.

"Hear, and I will speak: I will ask thee, and do thou tell me." (Job 42:4)

⊷ Pray that those in authority will act in accordance with God's will.

EVERYTHING BUT!

Not long ago Dr. Paul O. Carr, professor of history at Wilson Teachers' College, Washington, stated that when most people nowadays are asked for a description of democracy they are *"forced to fall back on our wage scales, our automobiles, our refrigerators, and ultimately and triumphantly to the American bathroom for their defense."*

The twentieth century indeed has brought unprecedented material progress, never even dreamed of by the emperors of old. Yet as material advantages and pleasures —good in themselves—have increased, *peace of mind and soul has decreased*. Even those with everything the world can give feel a lack of inner security. And this only serves to emphasize the point that the more a person makes pleasures of the body his constant aim, the more he is afflicted with frustration, unrest, and instability.

It is necessary to remember that man's soul is spiritual, made in the image and likeness of God. Do all in your power, then, to use the unsurpassed material advantages of our age—all gifts of God—for His glory and for the eternal, as well as for the temporal, welfare of mankind.

"Not by bread alone does man live, but by every word that comes forth from the mouth of God." (Matthew 4:4)

❧ Pray for an understanding use of this world's goods with a view to their value for the next.

YOU NEVER KNOW

"Do not forget to show hospitality; in doing this, men have before now entertained angels unawares." (Hebrews 13:2)

To most of us hospitality seems more a social grace than a real and positive virtue. We like to have our friends in, receive their compliments on our homes, our entertainment, our qualities as host.

But Our Lord is most specific about our duties to strangers, and it is good, from time to time, to remind ourselves of the great value of kindnesses to those unknown to us, especially if they are in need. We may not, it is true, be entertaining "angels unawares." But we may be spreading an influence for good, enacting Christ's message for someone who is ignorant of it, and in this direct way bettering the world by bettering those in it, helping those more unfortunate than ourselves.

"Ye are no longer strangers and foreigners, but ye are fellow citizens of the saints and members of the household of God." (Ephesians 2:19)

᪥ Help me, O Lord, to show true hospitality to all.

HE SHOWED HOLLYWOOD

A five-year-old refugee was recently being shown around a Hollywood department store by his American foster parents. When they came to the toy department, crowded with playthings in preparation for the Christmas rush, the little boy's eyes grew wide with wonderment. He examined the many items with amazed delight, but gradually the grownups noticed an expression of disappointment clouding the boy's face. He began to search up and down aisles, under tables, and behind counters. At last, when questioned what he was looking for, he burst out: *"But where is the Child?"*

There was an embarrassed silence. Then a store official gave instructions for a Christmas crib to be found at once and set up in a prominent place in the toy department. And at this the little boy smiled with delight. Young as he was, he had given a lesson in the real significance of Christmas. He had pointed out the grave oversight of overlooking the One for Whom the birthday party was being given!

"*. . . and a little child shall lead them.*" (Isaias 11:6)

⊷ Pray that you may carry the spirit of Christmas in your heart all through the coming year.

"THE HEART OF THE HOME"

Mrs. James F. McDonnell, a mother of fourteen children, and one person certainly who might have been expected to be so preoccupied with raising her large family that she would have no time for anything else, interrupted her busy schedule long enough to make these remarks before a representative gathering of women:

"The problems of juvenile delinquency, broken homes, unspiritualized education can only be solved by women. We know that at the very core and center of every so-called social problem lies the problem of the home. And the heart of the home is the woman.

"She is the creative unit of Society. What she makes of herself, and within herself, she makes of her family and of her home. Where there are love and truth and virtue and piety within her, they are within the walls of her home. But these things within her, nourished by Divine Grace, and cherished in human devotion, are never to be contained by walls. Her children take them from her, out into the world with them.

"So the woman who guards and guides the home sends forth men who alone are strong enough to guard all the other worthy citadels of the nation, and of civilization itself. Her spiritual inwardness creates all the outward triumphs of this world."

"Favour is deceit, and beauty is vain: the woman that feareth the Lord, she shall be praised." (Proverbs 31:30)

§ Pray that the example of the Holy Family will serve as a guide for *all* our homes.

THE REAL MEANING

Last year a friend sent us a beautiful Christmas card. The words across the top read: *"Peace on earth, good will to men."*

That sounds good, but actually is it the real meaning? The word-for-word literal translation of *"et in terra pax hominibus bonae voluntatis"* is *"and on earth peace to men of good will."*

That's something different, isn't it? But that's what the angels said, and that's surely what they meant. In other words, they wished peace to men who honestly want peace, who are *of* good will, but not to those of "bad will," the selfish, the cruel, the hateful, the impure.

As one thinker put it: *"When the men of good will outnumber those of ill will, the scoffers and infidels, the world will enjoy genuine peace and progress."*

"And suddenly there was with the angel a multitude of the heavenly army, praising God and saying: Glory to God in the highest and on earth peace to men of good will." (Luke 2:13-14)

꜅ Pray that God will move the hearts of those who are filled with ill-will, that they may turn to Him.

NO GETTING AWAY FROM IT

We always think of Christmas as something particularly regular and permanent. Yet it is a fact that in England, in 1644, Christmas was outlawed by an Act of Parliament. The day was declared a fast and a market day, shops were forced to stay open, plum puddings and mince pies were condemned as heathenish. There was resistance, of course, and even bloodshed; but after the Restoration Dissenters still called Yuletide "Fooltide."

In our own country we have many times passed "man-made" laws against our own best interests. In so many ways we try to dodge the truth, even though Christ keeps repeating that only *the truth shall make you free.*" No matter how hard men try to avoid it, eliminate it, or legislate it away, truth cannot be long suppressed. It has a wonderful resiliency; it never fails to snap back. As Bryant said: *"Truth crushed to earth shall rise again; The eternal years of God are hers . . ."*

"Heaven and earth shall pass, but my words shall not pass." (Matthew 24:35)

✍ Pray that you will make your voice heard whenever truth is at stake.

IT TAKES TIME

Once we watched some children plant seeds in a garden. We saw the careful attention with which they watered them. Then the next morning the children rushed to the window, expecting to see the garden filled with blooms. In their disappointment and impatience they proceeded to neglect the garden and finally the seeds died without ever having produced anything.

This simple experience can be an example to all Christophers not to be impatient of results. The true bearer of Christ does not expect his good work to bear immediate fruit. He does not expect to plant a seed and get a rosebush overnight. Indeed, he may labor at length and apparently in vain. But the truth is that he is winning all the time, because it is the labor itself that counts. As Paul said:

"I planted, Apollos watered, but God gave the growth. Consequently, neither is the planter anything, nor the waterer; but God who gives the growth." (I Corinthians 3: 6–7)

❧ Lord, help me to combine in myself good will, courage, and patience.

A QUICK CHANGE

Christ showed special regard for those whom we are inclined to shun. Zaccheus is a good example of our Lord's solicitude. In a few hundred words Luke tells the story of this publican, who climbed up a sycamore tree out of curiosity to see Jesus.

Jesus astonished the crowd and Zaccheus himself by saying: *"Zaccheus, make haste and come down; for this day I must abide in thy house."* (Luke 19:5)

Moved by this unexpected gesture of Christ, the rich sinner took immediate steps to make full amends to all he had wronged.

Often a surprise act of generosity or friendliness will melt the most frozen heart or move the most hardened sinner. All of us have known people, whom others found terrifying and austere, who were, we discovered for ourselves, only shy and afraid of being rejected. Real Christ-like affection is the surest letter of introduction, the always welcome gift, the most valid passport.

(*continued tomorrow*)

⋙ Pray for the wisdom and charity to see good even in the worst of people.

A QUICK CHANGE (*continued*)

There were a lot of factors against Zaccheus. He was rich, a sinner, and, worst of all, he was a publican, a tax-gatherer. Yet he climbed a tree to see Christ; out of idle interest, true—but interest, nevertheless.

When Christ singled out Zaccheus and sought his hospitality, the crowd murmured that He was consorting with a sinner. They openly disapproved of such an action: they wanted Him for *themselves,* as have many good people down through the centuries. But Our Lord went to Zaccheus's house, despite the censure of the throng.

The result? Zaccheus immediately caught the spirit of Christ and learned of Him the meaning of commutative justice. *"Behold, Lord,"* he exclaimed, *"I give half of my possessions to the poor. And if I have exacted money wrongfully from anyone, I restore it fourfold."* (Luke 19:8)

Our Lord's loving solicitude prepared the way for such a change of heart. Love accomplished in a matter of minutes what cold logic might never have succeeded in accomplishing.

"For the Son of Man is come to seek and to save that which was lost." (Luke 19:10)

⮕ Pray for the spirit of divine generosity.

NO GETTING AWAY FROM IT

In Chicago a young lady recently made this enlightening admission. *"You know,"* she said, *"for ten years I've been trying to convince myself that there is no God. But I've got to confess that in those ten years I haven't found one good reason for not believing in God."*

It further developed that this young woman had been tied up with the Communists for two years. She was anything but malicious. She was groping for the truth, but no one had made any attempt, she claimed, to reach her with it. On the contrary, she was being bombarded on all sides with atheistic, pagan, and materialistic ideas of all kinds. Knowing this, it is surprising that she has remained as good as she is. And because of this, also, her situation—and that of thousands like her—stands out as a challenge to us who know the truth and have not shared it.

There are so many people like this girl—groping, really groping for the truth. Yet too few are concerning themselves with giving them the truth. The ones who seem to bother with them most are those out to wreck the world. These people who are searching for Christ are much better disposed than most think. Kindness, patience, and genuine interest are the means a Christopher should use to show them the way to Christ.

"I am the way, and the truth, and the life. No man cometh to the Father but by me." (John 14:6)

ᕗ Pray for the millions groping for the Truth.

"THOSE POOR AMERICANS"

A missioner in China some time ago was telling a group of his poor Christians of a recent Mississippi flood disaster and the destruction and hardship it had brought about.

Though suffering as they were from war and famine, immediately his Chinese listeners were filled with sympathy. "Those poor Americans!" was their spontaneous reaction, followed by an offer to send a share of their food to the needy victims of the flood. With typical generosity they demonstrated once again the truth of an expression which is a popular one with millions of Chinese: *"all under heaven one family."*

How quickly most of man's troubles will disappear once enough people recognize that the one bond all men have in common is that each and every one comes from God and one day returns to God. When they realize that, then they will act with zeal and daring to bring back to Christ those millions who may never have heard His name. They will concern themselves with the physical welfare of others. But they will be even more solicitous about their eternal destiny.

"For I was hungry and you gave me to eat . . ." (Matthew 25:35)

⮞ Pray that you may have the true spirit of charity.